FLYCASTING
HANDBOOK

The author explaining the finer points of theory to a club seminar. These whole-day sessions have proved popular with angling clubs and are always well-attended by beginner and experienced alike, showing that however capable the angler, there is still the feeling that one's casting could be just that little bit better!
Photograph by courtesy of Windermere, Ambleside & District Angling Association.

FLYCASTING HANDBOOK

Peter Mackenzie-Philps

WARD LOCK

To the memory of my Father and Mother, who gave me a happy childhood, a love of the countryside and a recognition of the dignity of my fellow man.

To my wife Sue, whose unswerving loyalty and love is more than any man deserves.

To my sons Tony and Gordon, who still put too much effort into their casting, but whose growth into manhood has given me so much pleasure and pride.

And to my old fishing pals, Lambert Carmichael and Ewart Clay, both anglers of the old school who cast with their wrists, in whose company I have constantly been reminded that fishing is not just about catching fish, but that companionship, repartee and generosity of spirit are far more important.

Note: Lengths are given in yards and feet as these are still in use in the fishing world. We talk about a 9-foot rod, just as we still talk about a breaking strain of 4 lb.

Series Editor: Jonathan Grimwood

First published in Great Britain in 1991
by Ward Lock Limited, Villiers House,
41/47 Strand, London WC2N 5JE, England.

A Cassell Imprint

© Peter Mackenzie-Philps 1991

British Library Cataloguing in Publication Data
Mackenzie-Philps, Peter
Flycasting handbook.
1. Fly fishing. Casting
I. Title
799.12

ISBN 0–7063–6957–2

Typeset by Fakenham Photosetting Limited, Fakenham, Norfolk
Printed in Great Britain by The Bath Press, Avon

CONTENTS

ACKNOWLEDGEMENTS

The fellowship of the angling fraternity is usually unstinting in its help and guidance to others, and I have received a very fair share during my learning years. I am still in my learning years, and hope to remain so for a long time!

I owe a great debt to the late Dick Swift, whose patient teaching transformed me from an average angler into a good caster. My fellow members of the Association of Professional Game Angling Instructors have been generous with knowledge and shared experience despite the fact that, technically, we are competitors, and in particular I must thank Arthur Oglesby, Donald Downs, Howard Tonkin, Ken Smith, Eddie Hopkins and Sean O'Brien – good friends all.

The members of the British Casting Association welcomed me to several of their casting competitions and shared their knowledge with me as openly as they did with each other.

I should like to thank every single angler to whom I have ever given a lesson – I have learned from them all, if only that it is a mistake to be hidebound in one's approach to anything.

My great thanks to my friend MB, whose skill with a camera and dedication to perfection in his darkroom have produced nearly all the photographs in this book.

*   *   *

Fly casting is an art and a science, in which you can exhaust yourself, but never your subject.

INTRODUCTION

As I sit down at my electric typewriter to start work on my third book, I cannot help but reflect how life has changed since I first started fishing.

At about 5 years old, I caught my first trout. The scene was a family picnic on a sunny day in 1936 at a small reservoir on the moors near Glasgow. My mother, sitting on a travelling rug, was busy with a crochet needle. My father had two small children to entertain, and it did not take him long to organise a worm hunt and to beg some crochet thread and a couple of pins from Mum; soon my sister and I were lying on our tummies on the dam wall, peering into the tea-coloured depths where our crochet cotton, pins, and worms were suspended from trembling fingers. I can still vividly remember the ecstasy, the triumph, the hunter's killer instinct, call it what you will, with which I jerked that first fish soaring over my head into the grass behind me. I can still see its red and black spots, the butter yellow belly and the green gill covers. Perhaps 6 or 7 inches long, it was not just a trout. It was the start of a life-long passion which has kept me sane in times of trouble, has given me more friends, true friends, than any other hobby I can think of and, for a time, gave me a very good income when I was in the latter years of running my own tackle business.

That day, my sister caught more than I did. She continued to do so on almost every fishing trip we undertook together, whether it was for trout, or for mackerel in the sea! She puts it down to greater concentration. My excuse is that I spent more time at the oars than she did and, even though it must be 30 years since we last fished together, that is my excuse, and I am sticking to it!

Nowadays, I spend far more time teaching casting than I do actually fishing. My time seems to be in some demand for casting clinics at angling clubs, demonstrations at country shows, instruction at shows and company hospitality days, all quite apart from the hourly casting lessons I give. It has been brought home to me that the average British angler does not think he needs lessons – what is wrong with just grabbing a rod and going fishing? Slowly, however, as the cost of tackle rises, it is being appreciated that a lesson, or a couple of lessons, from a good professional instructor will transform the average angler into a good angler. After all, the same man, thinking of taking up golf for the first time, or tennis, or any other competitive sport, would automatically consider a lesson from a professional before venturing on to a golf course or tennis court.

I am a firm believer that it is more important to the average man to perform well at his hobby than it is to perform well at his job! If you doubt the truth of this statement, think of this – how often do you think of fishing while you are working at your job? Set this against the number of times you think of your job while you are fishing. See what I mean?

Almost everything about fishing can be learned from books. Of the many hundreds of fishing books written in this country in the last 50 years, there are perhaps ten really excellent ones. (These ten cover trout, sea-trout, salmon and grayling.) From these ten, one can absorb all the knowledge needed to be a reasonably competent angler, except for one aspect. That aspect makes or breaks one's performance in terms of fish caught. No matter how good one's knowledge of flies, insects, fish, weather patterns, boat-handling, tackle, knots, one puts up a sloppy performance if one cannot cast reasonably well. While there are a couple of excellent books on fly casting, they are both American, and do not in their entirety cover British tackle or conditions. I am not aware of an up-to-date book on casting which refers to British conditions, so I have decided to have a shot at writing one myself.

What are my qualifications for this task? Fifty-four years ago I caught my first trout. Not on a fly, I admit. My first fly-caught trout was only 46 years ago. I was taught by a lovely man who used to cut his rod on the first day of the season from a hazel clump, tie on a line of braided horsehair, wade in the river in a pair of old army boots, tie his flies in his fingers at the riverside, and charm wild brown trout out of that river in scores. My first rod was made of hickory wood, then I graduated to greenheart. I did not own a split cane rod until I was in my 20s, and shortly after that fibreglass rods were launched on the angling public, and I became the proud possessor of a Phillipson's Gold Band rod, sold by Farlows. I wish I still had that rod today – it was a beauty which threw a lovely line. In 1975 I started selling carbon fibre rods, being beaten by a couple of months by Dermot Wilson, bless him, whose tackle business at Nether Wallop became for me the symbol of honesty and fair dealing which I endeavoured to emulate.

Until I started my own tackle business in 1974, I was as untaught as the average angler, but I decided that, if I was to test and recommend tackle to my customers, I had better become qualified in some way. I had a shot at competition casting and decided it was not for me. Untaught as I was, I lacked the coordination necessary to cast prodigious distances, or with great accuracy. While I was treated as a welcome guest by many nice people, I just could not get the hang of it. I then contacted the Association of Professional Game Angling Instructors, and presented myself for the entrance exam. And failed.

I was then taken under the wing of Dick Swift. Dick was quite the most outspoken man I have ever met, totally honest in his comments about my casting, and after a year of almost-weekly casting lessons he pronounced me fit to enter again for the APGAI entrance exams. I can still remember the frustration I felt while I was struggling to emulate his effortless, flowing style of casting, and the comments he made to make me perform up to his demanding standards. I also remember his patience while he explained to me the finer points of a cast and then watched while I failed so often to turn his words into action. Dick worked hard on me, bless him, and when I finally stood on that lawn in York in front of Jack Martin, Arthur Oglesby and Howard Tonkin, and was told that I had passed, his grin of satisfaction seemed to lighten the grass. Dick died shortly afterwards – to my great regret. I have a great deal to thank him for.

At about the same time I entered myself for the tests run by the National Anglers Council, in conjunction with the Salmon & Trout Association, and passed as a Class One instructor for the NAC. So, by 1977, I was qualified by the two bodies in this country which are regarded as being able to measure the quality of angling tuition. I thought I knew it all!

At that stage I really started to learn. It was only after I had given a hundred or so casting lessons that I really felt I was getting to grips with the problems of teaching and fault-spotting. It is not enough just to know the theory. One has to be able to adjust the theory to cater for people of unusual build, people with special problems, like arthritis in a shoulder, or with fingers missing as a result of accident, people who cannot stand upright for long periods, people who are confined to a wheelchair; all these things, and many more, do affect the way a fly rod can be waved. Thirteen years after starting to teach, I think occasionally that nothing can surprise me any more – I have seen it all – and then a student turns up with a new way of expressing in words some muscular movement or rod movement, and I find I have learned again from a beginner. I have therefore learned not to be surprised any more, and I have realised that the day I think I really know it all is the day to give up, because I would not be a good teacher from that moment on. An open mind, and the ability to listen, are two attributes essential to the teacher of fly casting.

For those reasons, therefore, I must now say what I try to remember to say whenever I give a lecture on fly casting. *Everything I say from now on is my personal opinion*. I have my reasons for saying it, but I am quite prepared to be proved wrong by somebody who is better qualified than I am, or who has a better reason for his version than I have for mine.

I have studied many superb casters in action. I have read most of the books ever written on casting. I have watched and studied most of the video tapes on casting. And I was taught by Dick Swift, a master of the art. Far more important, I have taught perhaps several thousand people by now, and I have learned something from most of them. I have worked out, sometimes laboriously on pieces of paper, and sometimes as the result of a flash of inspiration, what I hope is a totally logical approach to the art of casting a fly. It is only simple mechanics, after all.

In the following pages I hope to show you how easy it can be. Happy fishing to you.

Peter Mackenzie-Philps
Deer Springs Cottage
Wetherby
Yorkshire

1
SETTING THE SCENE

Fly casting is not difficult. If it was difficult, I would never have mastered it, as I am a simple soul, not blessed with an elevated IQ rating. Anybody who has the coordination to change gear in a stick-shift car without fluffing more than occasionally can learn to cast a fly well.

Fly casting does not require huge muscles. Imagine that you have a flimsy wand in your hand, actually a long gentle spring, and if you cock the spring and allow it to uncock, it will throw the fly line all by itself. Yet one sees anglers doing gymnastics underneath fly rods in their attempts to cock the spring and allow it to uncock; I have heard this over-energetic style called casting like a berserk chimpanzee, but I do not think this is being fair to the chimps.

There are two golden rules about fly casting which, if firmly set in your mind, will help you to become a good fly caster. I shall discuss these rules in some detail, as they form the key to everything you are trying to do. The first rule is:

Without a good backcast, you cannot get a good forward cast.

This rule applies to every single cast you make with a fly rod, including the roll cast. There isn't a backcast part of a roll cast, I can hear you say. Don't you believe it – there is a backcast component in every single cast, as you will see when I come to talk about each of the casts and to break down their various movements.

The backcast positions the line, ready to be driven forward by the forward cast. If the backcast is in the wrong place, the forward cast will go to the wrong place, unless you have fighter-pilot reactions and build in a correction half-way through the casting sequence. If you are looking forwards, and concentrating on the fish, you will be unaware of what is happening behind you, and the bad backcast will have a disastrous effect upon the forward delivery.

For this reason, most of my teaching of beginners concentrates upon the backcast. If this goes well, the forward cast is easy to execute. If the backcast goes badly, the effects can be seen immediately the line arrives in the forward field of vision. The fault seen arriving out in front is so often blamed on faulty technique in the forward cast, whereas it is so often caused by faulty technique in the backcast. Sadly, the man trying to teach himself to cast, seeing the fault arriving out in front of him, tries to cure it

The size of this audience at the Chatsworth Angling Fair indicates the ever-present interest among anglers on the subject of fly casting. Lefty Kreh, from the United States, puts on a superb demonstration of line control.

by putting more effort into the next forward delivery. That doesn't go right either, so at the next attempt even more force is applied, and so it goes on, until the chap is tearing his underwear in his endeavours to cast an ounce of fly line 20 yards out over the water.

Walking round Swinsty Reservoir one day, I came across a pair of anglers. One of them, sitting on the bank, was trying to teach a raw beginner how to cast. The tyro was standing up to his knees in the water, and the waves were rolling out from his waders as he thrashed the rod back and forth. His pal, sitting comfortably behind him, said, 'Go on Charlie, give it more wellie, it will go'. Yet the poor man was almost at the hernia stage as it was. The line was whistling back and forth, and the fly, or the end of the leader (I do not think that there was a fly left on the end) was cracking on the stones behind him on every false cast. Finally, after perhaps a dozen false casts, there was a huge effort, accompanied by a banzai-like yell, and the line shimmied down in a heap about 8 yards out from the rod tip. I crept away, unable to bear the sight of all those fish being terrified, feeling at the same time desperately sorry for that beginner. Not only did he not have a clue, but the man trying to teach him was clueless too, and the likely outcome would be yet another angler who had a shot at fly fishing but who gave up because he could not get the hang of how to cast. For if he could not cast, he would be unlikely to catch anything, and never catching anything is the commonest cause of people abandoning our sport.

So please fix in your mind that a good backcast is the first step, and a most essential step, towards a good forward cast.

The second rule is:

The line will go where the tip of the rod goes, and the tip of the rod goes where your thumb goes.

I shall discuss in the next chapter how the rod is gripped, but it is sufficient to say here that your thumb should be on top of the grip. Look at your right hand, and extend it as if you were going to shake hands with somebody. Now curl the four fingers so that the tips touch the palm of the hand. You are now holding an imaginary fishing rod. Notice how your thumb is stuck out. Drop your thumbnail downwards, so that the thumb is pointing in exactly the same direction as are the bones of your forearm – you are now ready to think about putting a fly rod in that hand and making a cast. If you concentrate on where that thumbnail goes, you are ready to analyse correctly what is going to happen to that fly line.

It is particularly important that you concentrate upon that thumbnail if you have developed the bad habit of cocking the wrist back at the completion of the backcast. Imagine you have a fly rod in your hand. Close your eyes, do a backcast, and stop to let the line roll out behind you. Now open your eyes, and turn your head to look at your thumb. Is it higher than your ear? Is it out there sideways at full arm-stretch somewhere? Is it pointing back further than about 12.30? (Imagining that 12 o'clock is exactly upright.)

If any of these three questions are true in your case, you have a casting style which, at the very least, forces you to put more effort into your casting than is necessary and, at the worst, prevents you ever casting well. Do you want to do something about it? Then read on; once you have fixed this second rule in your mind – The line will go where your thumb goes.

I have mentioned effort, and it is time now to dispel some myths. Charles Ritz, in his fascinating book on fly fishing, suggests that a beginner should practise with a wine bottle filled with sand, and that it takes 100 hours of exercises to get the right arm into a fit state for casting. Frankly, this statement, cancelling out all the otherwise excellent theory, caused me to dump the book into my discard pile. I do not believe there would be many anglers out there today if they had all been told that they would have to do 100 hours of exercises before they could pick up a fly rod. Two-and-a-half working weeks waving a sand-filled wine bottle before I can try to catch a fish? No way, monsieur. Sorry.

Having said that, it does take muscular effort to wave a fly rod. It is here that I must digress into the world of advertising hype for a moment. Remember that, if a rod is described as 'powerful', it is you who supplies the power. The more powerful the spring, the more effort it takes to cock it. Of course, once it has been cocked, a powerful spring will deliver more power when it is uncocking itself and flinging the line. The question you have to ask yourself is – how 'powerful' a rod do you need? Luckily this question is answered for you by the rod maker, when he rates the rod by its AFTM number. The higher the AFTM number, the more powerful the spring, and the heavier the weight it will throw.

It is also true to say that the length of the rod has a great bearing on the amount of effort you have to put into casting with it. The longer the rod, the greater the leverage against you. It is this leverage against your muscles which will prevent you moving the tip of a long rod as fast as you would like. You don't believe me? Have you ever tried to cast with a 15-foot salmon rod, single-handed? Not many grown men can do it, and I can assure you it isn't just the weight of the rod which makes it so difficult. It is the fact that the weight of the line is hung out there perhaps 14 feet away from your grip. It is not an accident that competition casters have settled on rods around 9¼–9½ feet long for their distance rods. They know that distance is achieved by line speed. Line speed is a component of tip speed (plus, of course, double-haul technique) and it is ergonomically true that the man of average build finds maximum tip speed happening when he is waving a rod of around 9–9½ feet (single-handed of course). For men of slight build, women and small boys, this critical length is reduced.

So it takes effort to cock the spring of a fly rod. Not very much, I assure you. Stick the butt of a rod into the ground, or get a friend to hold it upright. Take hold of the fly line in the tips of your thumb and forefinger, perhaps 10 yards out from the rod tip, and pull gently until the tip is pointing at right angles to the butt. You will find that you are not having to apply much effort in those fingertips to achieve this state of affairs. Now let go the line, and the spring will uncock itself and fling the line to the far side of the rod. You have just gone through basically the same mechanics as when you cast a fly line – put all the line behind the rod, cock the spring, and let it uncock in the direction you want the line to go – simple, isn't it? *One word of caution.* Do not do this little experiment when you have a fly on the end! It is a certain recipe for a trip to hospital to get the hook dug out of your thumb.

Casting a fly takes so little effort, if it is done properly, that lightly built women can do it, boys of 10 years of age can do it, and doddery old men can do it. OK, you get tired after a while, so sit down and have a rest – admire the birds, look for rising fish, study the insect life, have a coffee. Fishing isn't about thrashing the water non-stop for 8 hours; you are there for fun, not for hard work. But those anglers who make hard work of their casting are not doing it properly, or else they are locked on to trying to cast out of sight all the time.

If you are casting well, and within your 'distance of delicate presentation', you will find that your feet get sore before your right arm does!

Casting does require muscular coordination. By this, I mean that your muscles must be able to do what your brain tells them to do. Among all the people I have taught to cast, there has been a great spread of ability to coordinate. If I may quote a simple example. Take a tennis ball, and throw it suddenly and without any warning to somebody, saying as you do so – 'Here, catch'. The reactions will vary, from the man who throws out his hand and has the ball stick as if by magic to his palm to the man who does not even see the ball go past him and has to have four shots at picking it up off the ground by his feet before he succeeds. At the one extreme we have people who are luckily so well coordinated that they become test pilots, county-class cricketers, or scratch golfers. At the other extreme we have those unfortunate people who walk into every second lamp-post. The difference is not something we have much control over, as it is an accident of birth, or heredity, or some physical damage in our nervous systems, but we can influence our performance to a degree by practice. I call this 'building in muscle memory'.

Muscle memory is something we all develop. It can be as simple as the fact that a smoker of many years always reaches into a certain pocket for his lighter, and on a beach will still unconsciously reach towards that same pocket even if he is wearing only his swimming trunks. Or the British beer drinker on his first visit to Germany who bashes his front teeth on the rim of a glass, because the handle is down near the bottom of the German glasses and in the UK the tankards have the handle fixed near the rim. Muscle memory tells him that the hand is raised to a certain point in front of the cheek in order to drink beer. Muscle memory is what makes it so difficult to overcome bad habits – the moment we stop thinking about what we are doing, muscle memory takes over, and we do something the way we always have done it, even if it is wrong.

Muscle memory is the reason why it is so essential that fly fishing starts with a lesson from a professionally qualified instructor – start by building in muscle memory for the right way and no bad habits are generated to cause grief later on. Quite apart from the understanding of what is required – it is obvious from a study of many anglers around our reservoirs that they do not understand what the line should do in the air, and how to

One of the author's pupils, Howard Croston, aged 14, fishing on the River Lowther. Already self-taught to a high standard, Howard needed only a final polish to his technique. As a result of subsequent dedicated practice, Howard won many casting competitions in 1990, among them Junior Trout Accuracy at Chatsworth; Trout Accuracy with Obstacles both Junior and Senior at the Game Fair; Trout Distance Junior, Salmon Distance Junior, and Trout Accuracy Junior at Lowther (where his scores in Accuracy and Victor Ludorum were higher than those of the winner of the senior sections!); and he rounded off the year by winning the Trout Accuracy, Junior and Senior, at the West Midlands Game Fair. The photograph shows a beautifully high straight backcast coming forward with a touch of left-hand haul to speed up the delivery of an accurate dry fly at long range – distance is often the key to catching wild brown trout. Photograph by courtesy of Paul Welch, of Tuffley, Gloucester.

The easy way to thread a rod. Double the leader back on the line, and thread the doubled end. If the leader and line slips, it jams in the last ring you threaded. And you can see and feel it better than you can a fine piece of nylon.

achieve this. How on earth can you correct a fault if you do not understand what causes it in the first place? Or even that it is a fault? I get the firm impression that the average angler thinks that, if a cast did not go right, the next one will if he puts twice as much effort into it! No wonder we see so many anglers lying asleep on the bank in the early afternoons – they will tell you they are waiting for the evening rise. If they told the truth, they would say that they have exhausted themselves in the morning, and need to have a rest in order to summon up the energy to drive home!

The ability to coordinate well is, I find, unusual in children under the age of 10 years. Of course, there is the odd exception, and I have taught a 6-year-old to cast a nice line in less than 15 minutes, but he was a very rare example of a future test pilot in the making. Most children lack the ability to learn the movements, or lack the muscular strength needed, until they are past the age of 10. Up to that age, they are best advised to stick to drowning worms – a very successful fishing method for a small boy or girl, who often catches more than Dad in the process. The ability to teach children is given to relatively few adults. I have heard expressions like 'Keep the line alive in the air, and then follow through' used to a small boy, who looked totally baffled, but who did his best, with poor results. When I whispered in his ear that he should stick his thumb in an enemy's eye, and the eyeball was on top of that tree, he grinned and made a beautiful forward cast! I told this story in my book on stillwater fishing, and one reviewer said that he thought it was a disgusting analogy – I gritted my teeth and wondered how the sensitive soul managed to bring himself to kill a fish! When one is teaching children, everything has to be expressed in terms which they understand clearly and, sadly, not many instructors have this ability to simplify their language to the comprehension level of a 10-year-old.

It should not be thought that only beginners need casting lessons. Some of the finest professional golfers will take themselves to another professional from time to time, to iron out small faults which creep in and spoil their performance, and which they cannot detect in themselves. This has become less necessary in these highly scientific days, when one can hire a video camera, set it up and film oneself, and then study at leisure, if needed in slow motion or frozen part-way through a swing or a cast. The first time I saw a video tape of myself in action, I was thunderstruck – I had developed faults, some of which, in students, are so basic that I start drawing pictures on pieces of paper. So the experienced angler should not feel shy at the prospect of a professional casting lesson – if you are enabled to perform even better at your chosen hobby, you will get much more satisfaction from it. Have you ever gone to a Game Fair and discarded the idea of watching the casting demonstrations because you know it all? If you have, you should not even be reading this book! If you are drawn to the casting demonstrations, you are, subconsciously perhaps, acknowledging that you still have something to learn.

Having set the scene before I start describing the various casts, and the technicalities involved, I will repeat the two basic rules which you must have fixed in your mind before we can go any further:

1) Without a good backcast you cannot get a good forward cast.
2) The line will go where your thumb goes.

Do you get the impression that this casting business is going to be easy to understand, and easy to do? I am going to try to make it easy to understand. Whether you can then pick up a rod and do it is entirely up to you – you are about to find out how well coordinated you are!

2
THE GRIP

Fishing is not a game where a score is kept. Golf and tennis are, and great emphasis is put on how to hold the club or racket. Believe me it is just as important how you start holding a fishing rod. An incorrect grip will affect your performance from the very beginning.

I am a great believer in the *KISS* principle (Keep It Simple, Stupid). If my fishing is made simpler, I am left with spare brainpower to concentrate on the fish and on what they are eating. Many of the tangles around the butt are caused in the first place by an incorrect grip, or rather they can be avoided by a correct grip. Every second you spend thinking about tangles around the reel or the butt is a second in which you are not thinking about fooling the fish. This is bound to be reflected in your catch rate, although you may never realise it. (You might be happy to average one fish a day!)

The following series of photographs shows the various grips I have seen used, and are accompanied by my comments upon them. For the sake of clarity, I have rolled my sleeves up – I would not like you to think I fish with bare arms when I am 'spring fishing' in February, when one can have snow up to the knees. Equally, when fishing the evening rise in Scotland in August, the fewer square millimetres of skin exposed to those eight-gun midges, the better.

Incorrect grip. No control over the rod, incipient wrist cocking, and line all over the place.

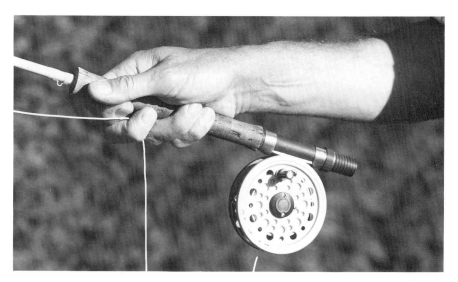

Thumb to the side of the cork. Still no control over the rod, position lacks power, line not under control.

Crooked thumb cannot push with any power, line not under control.

Forefinger lacks power to push, and the undergrip of only three fingers lacks power in the backcast. Acceptable with a tiny brook rod and only 20 feet of line, but ineffective for anything else.

Almost right. The way most anglers hold the rod. The grip is correct, but the line is not under control. Tangles around the reel are frequent. When retrieving the line, much stretching and reaching with the left hand is needed.

Correct grip. Line under control, fewer tangles around the reel. To retrieve line, pull with the left hand, inboard of the right forefinger – no need to keep reaching up to the butt ring. Only when a fish is hooked is the line released from the little finger.
It should be noted that all these photographs show a reel arranged for left-hand wind. There is no need to change hands when a fish is hooked.

3
THE STANCE

Much importance is placed by some instructors on the correct position for the feet and shoulders. Frankly I do not agree that stance is important, with one exception – when watching the backcast. Apart from this one exception, described below, the angler may find himself forced into various contortions while fishing – whether standing, upright or crouched down, kneeling, sitting in a boat, sitting in a wheelchair, or even wading up to the tops of chest waders with feet braced wide apart in a tearing current, although I must say that anybody who gets into this latter position had better be well insured!

The position of the feet is not important most of the time. How can one be dogmatic about foot position when kneeling down like this? This is a posed photograph – the author would never go fishing in a white shirt, or with his wallet hanging out of his hip pocket, or without eye protection!
In all the casting photographs in this book, there was no hook on the end of the leader, but a tuft of wool. If there had been a hook, every photograph would have shown sunglasses being worn!

Normally a stance with the right foot slightly forward gives a greater degree of comfort and control. However, if the head is turned to look at the backcast, the right arm automatically swings out to the side, and this puts a horizontal error into the path of the rod tip. You wouldn't punch somebody from this position, would you?

To watch the backcast, it is better to put the left foot forwards and to turn the shoulders sideways, left shoulder leading. The right hand, and thus the rod tip, can then track back and forth in a straight line, resulting in maximum accuracy and maximum power for minimum effort.

The most important consideration about stance is that one should be comfortable. I sometimes tell students to imagine that they are standing at a bus stop, they have been there for half an hour, and they are totally relaxed. Forget about the feet; face the way the bus will come from. While fishing, forget the feet, concentrate on the fish and on the action of the rod – nothing else is really important.

This is the one exception. (I shall describe in Chapter 4 how vital it is that the rod tip, and thus the thumb, tracks back and forth in a straight line.) If you turn your head to watch the backcast, and you are not standing sideways to your target, the right arm will inevitably swing out sideways at the extremity of the backcast. This carries two penalties – the backcast will have a horizontal error in it, and the muscles which pull the hand forward from this position are much smaller than the muscles which punch forward from the ball of the shoulder. By using smaller muscles, you will have to make them work harder than you would larger ones, and you will tire more quickly. To watch the backcast, therefore, it is essential that your left foot is forward, and your shoulders turned sideways on to the target, left shoulder leading.

If, however, you do not need to watch the backcast (and once the timing is grooved into your subconscious you will not have to), you can stand any old way you like, so long as you are comfortable and have control over the arm which is holding the rod. For fishing with a double-handed rod, or for double-hauling with a trout rod, you need control over both arms.

The correct way to walk down to the waterside. Rod pointing backwards, tip high, reel downwards.

The way too many anglers do it – and then weep salt tears when they walk the tip into the ground or into a tree!

4

THE OVERHEAD CAST WITH A TROUT ROD

Let us start by establishing what we mean by certain terms. During much of our discussion on casting, reference will be made to times like 9 o'clock, 12 o'clock, and so on. So that there can be no confusion, I want you to imagine that you are standing against a large clock. Your right ear is next to the pivot for the hands. You are standing upright, but relaxed. If I refer now to 12 o'clock, I refer to a position directly above your head. If I talk about 9 o'clock, I am referring to a position straight out in front of you, at a height level with your ear. 3 o'clock is directly behind you, also at the height of your ear. Please study the clock-face picture opposite to see exactly what I mean, bearing in mind that the pivot for the hands of the clock, the starting point for all the directions denoted by the time, is *the right ear*. If you prefer to think of this starting point as your right eye, I would not argue with this, as the eye and the ear are both approximately the same height from the ground.

You will notice that the radius of the clock face (roughly the length of the minute hand) is about 8 feet so that, if the right thumb is stopped right beside the ear, and the thumbnail is about 1 foot from the butt button of the rod, the tip ring of the rod will be touching the number 12. (Assuming that we are using a 9-foot rod.)

To prevent any possibility of confusion, I will say here and now that many writers about casting visualise the hands of the clock as pivoting on the right elbow or on the reel of the rod. While I would, with a smile, suggest that some of these writers do not know their ear from their elbow, I must stress that the hands of *my* clock are pivoted on your right ear. If you are a left-hander, sorry, but you will by now have realised with a sigh that you are going to have to translate everything into corrie-fisted language.

The overhead cast is the commonest cast. It is also mechanically the most efficient cast, yielding greatest distance for least effort. It is the cast used by the majority of anglers all the time, and not necessarily because they know no other. The overhead cast yields greatest accuracy, greatest delicacy of presentation, and is perhaps the easiest cast to perform well.

Before the overhead cast is started, it is essential that the fly line is laid out straight on the water in front of you, with little or no slack in it. There should be no slack inboard of the butt ring either, so any loose line inboard of the butt ring should be held tightly in the left hand, or trapped under a finger of the rod hand. I am often asked how one gets the line out there, lying straight, in the first place, and this is an extremely good point. Let us start by imagining that you are in the car park, tackling up at the beginning of the day.

Tighten up the reel fitting, so that there is no possibility of the reel dropping off into 50 feet of water. Check that the spigot joints are tight. (You did rub the male spigot with a white wax candle, didn't you? This avoids wear on the spigots, and prevents the tip flying off half-way through a day's fishing.) You are an idle angler, and the leader from the last trip is still attached to the line, and you did remember to leave 6 inches of leader point sticking out from the reel, so that you do not have to dig around to find the end, which always goes coil-under-coil on the spool! Pull a few yards of line off the reel, double the leader and line so that you thread the leader/line joint through the rings. I always smile when I see anglers peering and poking to thread the tip of the leader up through the rings. Sod's Law says that when they get to the tip ring, it slips from their grasp and leaps back down the rod, so that they have to start all over again. I usually put my fingers in my ears when this happens, as my Mum told me that all that terrible language was bad for me. By doubling the line and leader, and threading the doubled end, it jams in the last ring I threaded if it does slip, and because it is fatter and more easily seen, it is less inclined to slip in the first place.

Pull several feet of line out through the tip ring, glance along the rod to ensure that you haven't missed a ring, and reach for your spool of nylon to put a new tippet on the leader. Are you using the same tippet as you used last week? Then you deserve to get broken on the first fish. Get your flybox out, and select a fly – although the cunning angler leaves this last action until *after* he has been down to the edge of the water and seen what flies are around. If you do tie the fly on in the car park, check the knot well, and then hook the fly on one of the intermediate rings on the rod, as far away from the handle as you can reach comfortably. Do not use the tiny thing, euphemistically called a keeper ring, just in front of the cork handle. Bring the leader back round the reel, and wind up tight. You will thus have achieved three things. You will have avoided the line/leader joint coming

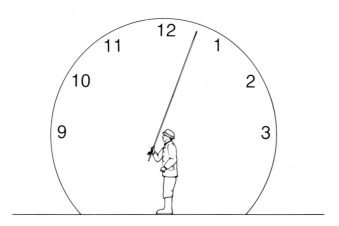

25

back through the tip ring, so it will not jam when you want to start fishing and try to pull it out. By avoiding this joint coming back through the tip ring, you will avoid putting a kink in the leader material where the leader doubles back over a sharp angle – this kink can stay in all day and drive you mad. And, lastly, when you carry your rod down to the waterside, carrying it pointing backwards by the point of balance, you will not get a fly stuck in the palm of your hand. I always carry my rod pointing backwards – the last rod I walked into a tree was many years ago. Pointing backwards is much kinder to the bank balance. I hold the tip of my rod up high behind me, though, so that my companion does not stab his eye out on it, and reel down, so that, if I do walk under low branches, the rod is just stroked out of the way, and the rings are not knocked off as they would be if the reel was on top.

Arriving at the waterside, a rod-length from the water, take the fly off that intermediate ring up the rod, unloop the leader from the reel, and flick the fly onto the water. Pull some more line from the reel, perhaps two rod-lengths, and, holding the rod pointing downwards, waggle the tip gently from side to side, at the same time guiding the slack into the butt ring with the left hand. The line slides out through the rings, and is now lying on the water in front of the tip ring. Draw the rod slowly back, and do a roll cast. This takes all the line out, and it is now lying straight in front of you, ready for the first overhead cast. (We shall cover the technicalities of the roll cast in Chapter 16. For the time being, please believe me when I say that it is the easiest way to get the line out there in the first place.)

First, the theory. The overhead cast is meant to be just that – overhead. Too many anglers suffer from what I call the 'Dog Nobbler Duck', where they shrink their necks every time the forward cast is delivered. They do this because of their habit of bringing the rod back sideways and forwards over the top. This drops the backcast low, so it will come forward low, and a heavy fly will try to knock their head off. If the backcast stayed high, and everything rolled over the tip of the rod, both in the backcast and in the forward cast, that heavy fly would never come nearer than 9 feet, and they would not all look like alarmed tortoises ducking their heads into their collars every cast.

The line will travel fastest if it rolls over the top of the rod. This is much faster than if it rolls beside the tip ring or lower than the tip ring. The faster the line travels, the farther it will go. In order to make the line roll over the top of the rod, it is essential that the tip ring tracks back and forth in the same plane, straight backwards, and straight forwards. Forget about putting that deliberate ellipse into your casting – where you track backwards in a different plane from the forward cast – this costs you distance, or effort, or both.

For greatest safety, however, it is wise not to start your casting career with the rod absolutely vertical. If you do get a low cast, it will embed a fly in your face, or in the back of your neck. Better to lean the rod slightly to the right, so that at the extremity of the backcast, a plumb line from the tip of the rod would just clear your right shoulder. Don't worry. Your line will still go over the tip of the rod, however; it is just that the rod is leaning very slightly to the side.

Now to the cast itself. The overhead cast has, in its basic form, five components.

The lift

If you start the power of the backcast immediately, you will snatch the line from the water, leaving a line of foam along the surface. There will be no fish left under that line of foam – they will have fled in panic. The whole idea of fly fishing is that you are throwing artificial food to fish. If they are in the least alarmed, the first thing they will do is to stop eating. So it pays not to frighten them by snatching the line from the surface. Glide it off the water by lifting the rod tip gently, until the rod points to 10 o'clock. As you lift the rod tip, you will see the line sliding along the surface towards you – moving line is gripped less by the surface tension of the water than is a stationary line, so you have also helped to 'unstick' the surface tension. Do *not* lift the rod tip by bending the wrist. Bend only the elbow. The butt button should still be touching the underside of your arm.

The lift should start when the tip ring is touching the water, and with no slack under it. By starting the lift as low as possible, you give the line maximum movement by the time the tip reaches 10 o'clock. If you had started with the tip ring a yard above the water, you would not have moved the line much by the time the tip ring reached the critical 10 o'clock position. Do not hurry the lift – the slower you lift, the less disturbance of the water, and the fewer fish you frighten. About 2 seconds is, I find, an average time for the lift to take, and that is a surprisingly long time. The split second that the tip of the rod reaches 10 o'clock, you are ready to accelerate the tip into . . .

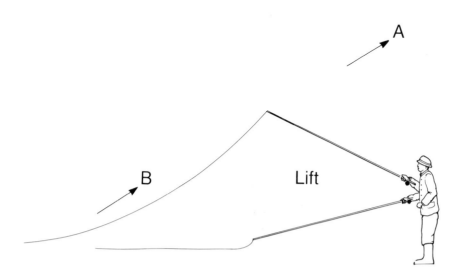

If the rod starts with the tip almost touching the water, and lifts only to 10 o'clock, the tip will flick backwards and upwards in the direction of arrow A; the line being driven in the same direction, arrow B. The backcast will thus go safely over the angler's head.

If the lift is started high, the flick will be too far back, driving the line downwards, in the direction of the arrow. If the line sags, it will be driven back into the caster's face, or the fly will hit the rod in the backcast.

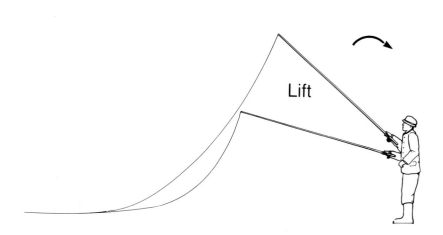

Lift

The flick

This is where you make the top half of the rod act like a little spring. There are several ways of describing the correct movement of the flick, and some will be better understood than others. I have heard it described as flicking a piece of mud off the tip ring, in a skywards direction behind the rod. I have heard it described as flicking water off a paintbrush, so that the water leaves the tip ring vertically. I have heard that you should hold an imaginary hammer in your hand, and tap a nail beside your right ear. Whatever analogy works best for you, the important thing is that you flick the tip of the rod to drive the line upwards into the air, high behind you. Think of it as an upcast, not a backcast. (See A.)

One of the commonest casting faults is not making the tip of the rod flick. Instead a great sweep of the rod is made, hardly bending the spring at all, and the result is always a weak backcast which, because of its lack of line speed, usually drops low behind. A low backcast causes hooks to be broken on the ground behind you, and will use up much of the energy of the forward cast in climbing back over the tip of the rod. A high backcast, at least as high as the rod tip, has only to run downhill on the forward cast, and is thus as mechanically efficient as possible.

Think of that little flick. It takes the line from low in front of you, and puts it high in the air behind you. This involves more energy that does the forward cast running downhill. So that little flick should be the most powerful part of the whole casting sequence. Many beginners do what is called in Yorkshire 'drawing back and giving it one', where far more effort is put into the final delivery, and not nearly enough into the preliminary flick upwards and backwards. The result is that they never achieve a good backcast – remember rule number one – and thus never achieve a good forward cast either.

The flick is put into the rod tip by the muscles of the arm; to be precise, by the biceps, and by the biceps alone. This muscle is the one which bulges above the elbow when you clench your fist with your elbow bent. (The biceps is on the front of the arm; it is the triceps which is on the rearward side of the arm.) It is a mistake to try to put the flick in by using any wrist movement. The muscles of the wrist are not strong enough to do it properly, and you will complete the flick with the wrist cocked back. The wrist must end up still cocked downwards, with the button of the rod still touching the underside of the forearm, or nearly touching. In other words, during the whole of the lift and the flick, the rod is pointing in the same direction as the bones of the forearm. The rod must be an extension of those bones – the minute the rod deviates from the direction of those bones, the backcast will go wrong. (See B.)

How strong should that little flick be? Just enough to make the line flow out behind the rod tip and stop. There should be no shock waves in the line caused by a vibrating rod tip. Obviously, the more line you have extended, or the heavier that line is (higher AFTM number), the more effort it takes to make it all roll out high behind the rod tip, but it is a common fault to put too much effort into the flick and to leave the tip of the rod vibrating like a tuning fork, sending waves along the fly line as it does so. (See C overleaf.) Use just enough power to make the line roll out and for the leader and fly to turn over, leaving line, leader and fly all hung out in a straight line behind the rod tip, and at least as high as the rod tip.

A very common fault is to put so much power into the backcast that, although the butt of the rod is stopped at 12.30, the tip will carry on in a kick downwards and throw the line downwards behind you. Too much effort, and you will be unable to stop the tip smoothly. (See B again.)

Where should the flick go to? It started as the rod tip reached 10 o'clock, remember, and accelerated the tip ring upwards and backwards from there. The flick should end as the thumb arrives beside your ear, or in front of the ball of the shoulder. To be precise, I prefer to see the thumbnail stopping beside the lobe of the ear. If you do this, and the button is still

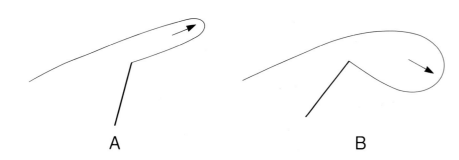

A   B

Starting with the line straight
out in front of you, with no
slack under the rod tip . . .

. . . Start a slow lift of the rod
tip . . .

touching the underside of your forearm, the rod will have stopped at 12.30, no later. If you look at the clock-face drawing on page 25 and draw a line from 10 to 12.30, you will see that the tip ring has had to track *upwards*. Thus the backcast will go upwards, and that is exactly what you want to happen.

You started the whole casting sequence with the elbow bent at slightly more than a right angle, rod tip touching the water. You lifted until the tip ring reached 10 o'clock and, during this lift, the elbow, although it bent, did not move from its position beside your waist. Then the rod was accelerated into the flick, and the elbow bent even more to put the flick in. The elbow might move *forward* a couple of inches during the flick, and it might move *upwards* by an inch at most, but it should not move more than this. *I do not mean that you should put a book under your upper arm to immobilise it* – the inevitable consequence of this is a wristy action and a low backcast, and many unfortunate anglers have been taught this fault by well-meaning and

. . . Until the tip of the rod comes to 10 o'clock. At that point, and no later, start an acceleration into a flick upwards and backwards.

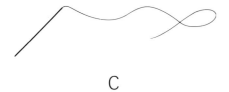

C

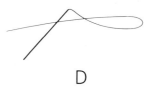

D

ill-informed friends. It is essential that the upper arm is free, but it should not move much in the backcast.

Having started the flick, it is important to realise that the line is still all in front of the tip ring. The tip ring is hauling the line back in a straight pull, overcoming the surface tension of the water and the weight of the line, leader and fly. It is not until the flick stops that the line starts to roll over the tip ring and go behind the rod.

The pause

It takes a surprisingly long time for the line to roll out high and straight behind the rod tip. Most beginners are amazed at how long they have to wait, but having asked the question – 'How long should I wait?', and been told that the answer is 'How long is a piece of fly line?', I encourage them to watch the line in the air behind them. Remember that, if you are going to watch the backcast in the air, it is essential that your left foot and left shoulder are forward, pointing towards the target (see Chapter 3).

How the line behaves in the air while you are pausing is very largely dependent upon the track and speed of the rod tip during the flick, and whether it stopped gently at the completion of the flick. Providing the tip ring is kept absolutely stationary during the pause, nothing else can influence the line during the pause, except perhaps a howling gale.

Right at the beginning of the pause, immediately the rod tip stops, the line rolls over the top of the rod. This is sometimes described as 'forming the loop' and this term rolls off the tongue of some instructors to the total bafflement of new students. I tend to explain that a long thin U-shape, with the U lying on its side, rolls along the line all the way from the tip ring to the fly. I then show this unrolling loop with a piece of string on a table-top, and comprehension is seen to dawn. I then describe the difference in streamlining between a narrow loop and a wide loop, and how the narrow loop will go further for less effort, and so my students tend to pick up a fly rod knowing beforehand what the line should look like in the air, and the movements needed to achieve a good cast. See A & B on page 29.

If the flick is not powerful enough, the line will not roll out straight before it starts to drop under the influence of gravity. Actually it starts to drop as soon as it starts to move, just as a rifle bullet starts to drop the moment it leaves the muzzle, but for the purposes of this discussion I mean that it starts to drop when it runs out of backward momentum. The angler, seeing his line beginning to fall, and realising that he had better be quick or the fly will catch on the grass behind him, starts the forward cast. At this moment the fly is still going backwards. The result is a crack noise, as the fly goes around the corner at over 720 miles an hour, roughly the speed of sound at sea level, the tippet cannot stand the strain and breaks, and the fly ends up in the next county. The angler then fishes away for the next hour with a blissful smile on his face, totally unaware that there is no fly on the end, and that he is there only for the exercise! A size 14 dry fly, cracked forward like this, has quite enough inertia to break 6-lb nylon quite often, and 4-lb nylon every time.

A crack or click noise on the backcast usually means that there is no fly on the end – stop and check immediately.

With the rod passing through the 11 o'clock position, still flicking upwards and backwards. (This is where some anglers start the backwards flick – see Chapter 10 on casting faults.)

Now stop the rod at 12.30. It does not matter if the butt leaves the forearm by a little, so long as the rod stops at 12.30. Note that all the line is now moving upwards and backwards, under tension, being pulled by the tip ring.

Once the rod stops, the line can roll over the tip ring and start forming the loop. Note that – provided the tip ring stops in the correct place – the loop will travel also upwards and backwards.

For safety's sake you can lean the rod slightly to the right, like this, so that a low cast either forwards or backwards will not stick the fly in you!

What, therefore should you be doing during the pause? The simple answer is *nothing*. You are merely waiting for the line to roll out straight behind the rod tip. I know that some people say you wait for the tug. I have read some magazine articles which say that you wait for the rod to load, and both of these expressions are rubbish, again said by well-meaning people who do not understand the finer points of casting.

If you get a tug at the extremity of the backcast, it signifies that the line has had to be forcibly stopped from going back any farther. It wanted to go farther, but the rod stopped it. In other words, you, holding the rod, stopped it. But why put the extra effort into the cast in the first place? It reminds me of the driver who accelerates fiercely then has to stamp on the brakes at the traffic lights, instead of just coasting to a stop. Wasted energy in both cases, one provided by petrol, the other by your breakfast. I am a great believer that fly casting should not waste energy – put into it only what is needed, and save the rest to give your wife a cuddle when you get home. So the people who say they wait for the tug are wasting energy. If the line just coasts to a stop up there you do not feel a thing.

Equally, people infer that the rod is loaded by the line going backwards. If this was really true, they would not have to do a forward cast. The loaded rod would merely have to be allowed to unload, and the unloading should do the forward cast. What they are really doing is loading the rod twice, once at the end of the backcast and again in the forward cast, and that wastes energy. The only time this is a good idea is during a casting competition, when you are trying to put the fly in the next county, but do

For extreme accuracy you can bring the rod to your forehead, like this. If you do so, you may well have been taught by the late Jack Martin. Jack taught this style not necessarily for accuracy alone, but because if you do cock your wrist you ding yourself on the head. A beautifully simple way of making a beginner stop the rod upright in the backcast.

you approach your fishing as if it were a distance-casting competition? No wonder you have to have a sleep on the bankside in the afternoon!

At the end of the pause, the line has all flowed out straight, no wiggles or waves in it, and it is all at least as high as the tip ring of the rod. The rod is frozen at the 12.30 position, your brain says 'Now', and you start . . .

The push

This is otherwise known as the forward cast, but as the forward cast has two components, not one, I shall call it the push. There are those who say that to push the arm out during the forward cast is wrong, and that this causes wind knots. I hope to show you that pushing the thumb out to full arm-stretch is, from a mechanical point of view, the only correct thing to do.

To achieve a powerful drive outwards of the rod tip, you have to produce a powerful drive outwards with the thumb. Equally, maximum power is given to the fly line if the rod tip moves in a straight line. To move the rod tip outwards in a straight line, it is essential that the thumb moves in a straight line, and that the straight line commences from beside the ear – that is where the thumb froze while the pause took place.

The desired angle of projection is not downwards towards the water. This would result in the line landing very hard on the surface, probably before it has become fully extended. The target area for the arrival of the fly is perhaps 1 foot above the surface, at a distance from your feet resulting from the combined lengths of your arm, the rod, the line and the leader. For example, my arm is about 2 feet long, the rod is 9 feet, the fly line is, say, 30 feet and the leader is 9 feet. This gives a grand total of 50 feet. So the

The rod has been frozen at 12.30 like this for over a second, until all the line has rolled out behind. The split second it is all straight . . .

... The thumb starts the forward push to cock the spring. As the rod tip dips slightly in the cocking movement, the line near the tip dips slightly in the air. The first few feet of the line start to drop anyway while the caster waits for the tail end of line and leader to roll out.

The forward push completed, thumb turned down, and the forward loop formed and rolling out. Note the leader and fly coming through at least 6 feet above the caster's head.

fly should land about 50 feet from my toecaps, providing everything is straight. Any wiggles in the line will reduce the distance.

Assuming I am not shooting any loose line, at the moment I started the forward cast, the fly was approximately 40 feet behind me. (My arm was not extended backwards, so deduct 2 feet. The rod was pointing to 12.30, the tip being perhaps a foot back behind the vertical, so deduct a further 8 feet.)

Thus the fly has to travel a total of 90 feet between the extremity of the backcast and its forward landing zone. During that time, gravity will exert its influence on the line, leader and fly, and I will therefore have to compensate for this by aiming slightly higher than a line-of-sight to the target. In other words I have to give it a little trajectory. I do not drive my thumb directly at the landing zone, but above it. How much higher I aim is dependent upon whether I want the fly to hover before landing (into a headwind I do not want this – see Chapter 6), how far I am trying to cast, the weight of the line, and the weight of the fly. The trajectory of a 3–inch brass tube fly at the end of 30 yards of DT 12 fly line will be very much higher than that of a size 14 dry fly on the end of 10 yards of DT 4 fly line, to quote two extremes. Before any ballistics expert writes to me, let me say that the height of the trajectory is very much influenced by the speed of the projectile, I know, but, in casting, one is driving the line as fast as the spring of the rod will flick it anyway; variations of speed can therefore be ignored when all I am trying to do is to establish that the line has to be fired off in a direction above the horizontal so that it goes as far as you want it to before it lands, and lands as lightly as possible.

We have, I hope, agreed that the line has to be projected above the horizon in front of us, thrown by the spring of the rod. But the spring has to be cocked before it will throw the line. How do we cock the spring?

Some people suggest that this is done with a flick of the wrist. The snag here is that small muscles flick the wrist, and small muscles will scream in protest after a while. They are just not up to the demands of casting all day. Other people say that the forearm should be tapped forward, just like using a hammer on a nail in front of you – their illustrations show the arm still bent when the hammer blow is completed. There is a grave defect to both the wrist flick and the hammer tap. They both tend to jerk the rod tip forward, and to stop it suddenly. The sudden stop causes a vibration of the rod tip, which sends a wave down the fly line. When the wave gets to the end, the fly flicks back and either hooks onto the line or leader, or goes through the tailing loop it made, and ties a wind knot. Wind knots are caused by jerky movements of the rod tip, in turn caused by jerky muscle movements. To avoid wind knots and tangles (both in the backcast and in the forward cast) the rod must be made to move smoothly. Yet at the same time we have to cock the spring and allow it to uncock.

Imagine your right thumb started off from beside your ear and, in a long gentle but firm push, ended up at full arm-stretch out in front of you. This is the movement made by that small boy when I told him to 'stick your thumb in his eye'. It is also the movement one would make if asked to flick the water off the bristles of a paintbrush and land the water as far away as possible (although there is a danger with the paintbrush analogy of a

The rod settled down, aimed well above the water, and the line flowing out in front, almost ready to hover a few feet above the water and settle like thistledown.

As the line settles with a sigh on to the surface, the tip is followed down until within a hand's breadth of the surface. Thus there is no slack under the rod tip after the line has landed. The overhead cast has been completed with minimum effort. It should be noted that this series of photographs was taken showing a cast of 12 yards of line, plus 3 yards of leader being cast with a 9-foot rod. The fly was therefore landing 18 yards (54 feet) away.

degree of wrist-flick being used, so that we would suffer wind knots in consequence). It is also the movement resulting from the suggestion that one reached out and put the tip ring of the rod into the top of that tree on the horizon. One could also say that the thumb is on a runner attached to a curtain rail, one end of which is attached to the right ear – run the thumb along the curtain rail until you run out of arm.

It will be noticed that all of these simple analogies result in the same thing – the arm is pushed out to full arm-stretch, so that the thumbnail tracks as far as possible from its starting point beside the ear. So the rod tip is propelled under power for as long as possible. Power applied over a long time is more total power, yet at any one split second less effort is being put into the job.

Power applied in a short concentrated jab, as in the wrist-flick or the hammer blow, has to be jerky, and has to involve the muscles in more effort, even though it is over a shorter time span. I have met one angler who cheerfully admits that after his first fishing trip each season he takes a week off work while his inflamed wrist settles down! If he had used the triceps muscle instead of the little wrist muscles he would not have suffered any pain at all.

The push, therefore, is a long firm movement, starting with the right thumb beside the right ear and ending with the thumb out as far in front as one can comfortably reach, and aimed along a line of sight slightly above the horizontal. At this stage I must stress that, once one becomes proficient at fly casting, many of these muscle movements become abbreviated, or streamlined a little, for the sake of smoothness and the involvement of least effort. However, if you learn the slightly exaggerated movements as I have described them, your casting will go well. If you start by learning the abbreviated movements, and then shorthand them, you will find that you are having to put a conscious effort into each cast, in the form of a wrist-flick, and you will start to get wind knots.

The result of the push is that the line flows out, above the water, until it is fully extended, then the leader flows out, and finally the fly hovers above its landing zone, perhaps a foot above the water. I will describe in Chapter 10 the symptoms and causes of the faults which will prevent this desirable state of affairs.

The drift down

Imagine you have completed the push. The fly hovers, and then the fly, leader and line drop about a foot and land gently on the water. Your rod tip is still several feet above the water, out at full arm-stretch, and you do not move. The immediate effect will be that the line sags below the rod tip, hanging vertically, and as it does so, the whole of the line will be drawn along the surface towards you. So will the leader, and so will the fly. Real flies do not land and slide along the surface, they land and sit still. You are therefore less likely to get a rise to your fly, because it has behaved unnaturally.

If you had followed the line down with the rod tip, so that, as the fly landed the rod tip also touched the water, your fly would have behaved as the natural does, landing and sitting still. Your line would all be lying along the surface in a straight line, so your fly would be several feet further away from you than if it had slid along the surface under too high a rod tip. A high rod tip costs you up to 2 yards of distance.

There is another disadvantage to fishing with the rod tip too high above the water, with a sag of slack line hanging vertically below it. When a fish is seen to take the fly, you strike. Quite apart from the fact that a strike can vary between a little flick of the wrist and a great wrenching heave (frequently accompanied by pulling line down through the butt ring with the other hand!) – let's just say you strike. Because there is slack line hanging below the rod tip, it is this which starts to move first in response to the strike. This slack line gathers momentum, and so does the rod tip, quite independently of the line and leader. These move last, driven by the momentum you gave the slack. When everything comes up tight, with the hook in the fish's jaw, there is a ping, and the tippet breaks. If, on the other hand, you had followed the line down with the rod tip, there would have been no slack under the rod tip and, on the strike, all the line would have started to move at the same time, cushioned by the shock-absorbing effect of the rod tip. The tippet would not have broken unless you really overcooked the strike to a ridiculous degree.

The drift down involves drawing the thumb down and back, from its 'thumb in his eyeball' position, to the position you would adopt when shaking hands, with the right elbow down around the waist. And that is where we started the whole casting sequence. You are again totally relaxed, ready to concentrate upon that fly out there, and on the fish which is just about to try to eat it.

Easy, isn't it? All we did was to remember that the line goes where the right thumb goes. We therefore tracked the right thumb upwards in the backcast, and outwards in the forward cast. The result was poetry in motion as the line flowed out, the fly hovered and landed like thistledown, and a great trout took it the second it landed.

*   *   *

Everything I have said in this chapter applies in conditions of still air, or with the wind blowing from my left to my right. In the next two chapters I shall describe the variations needed to cope with adverse winds.

In a following wind, unless it is a full-blown gale, no variation is needed. A stiff wind might tend to stop the backcast rolling out nicely, but this can be cured by giving slightly more flick in the rod tip as it drives the line back. You could also try doing a single-haul (see page 47). In a very strong following wind a single-haul becomes desirable.

5

THE OVERHEAD CAST – Wind from the Right

It is a recipe for disaster to cast over the right shoulder if there is more than the gentlest of zephyrs blowing from your right. A low cast, and we all get one occasionally, will be blown at you, and you are in the gravest danger of getting a hook in the face or the back of the neck. This is a bad idea, as you would find yourself in the queue at the local hospital casualty department, where the duty doctor will scratch his head, send for the electrician's wire-cutters, wreck your fly by cutting the barb and point off, and then puncture you twice more, once in each cheek of your rear end – once for anti-tetanus and once for penicillin. You end up feeling thoroughly punctured, I assure you. Best to avoid all that nastiness by never sticking a hook into yourself by bad casting.

If the wind is blowing from your right to your left, there is only one safe place for that fly to travel back and forth – on your left-hand side, or downwind of you.

I have read a book which suggests that it is correct to stand with your back to the water, putting your forward cast overland, and landing your backcast on the water behind you, turning around to fish out each cast. This is such a ridiculous suggestion that I was outraged that somebody should set himself up as an authority and tell poor unsuspecting beginners such rubbish. Bad enough that some self-taught anglers should do it this way, and I have to admit that I see an occasional angler casting great distances using this method, but for an instructor to suggest that this is the correct way to do it is a bit much. Needless to say he was not a member of the Association of Professional Game Angling Instructors. All that turning around also screws one's feet into the mud so that there is a risk of falling over when one wants to move!

I have also seen it written as if on stone tablets that one should be ambidextrous, training oneself to cast equally well with the left hand as with the right. May I say that I am strongly right-hand-oriented, and find the greatest difficulty in doing anything with my left hand, let alone casting all day.

There is an easier way to overcome the problem. Hold the rod in the right hand, as normal. In the backcast, take the right thumb to the left ear instead of to the right ear. The line will then track back and forth on your left side, downwind and safe.

A slight variation is necessary if the cast is to go really well. Before the

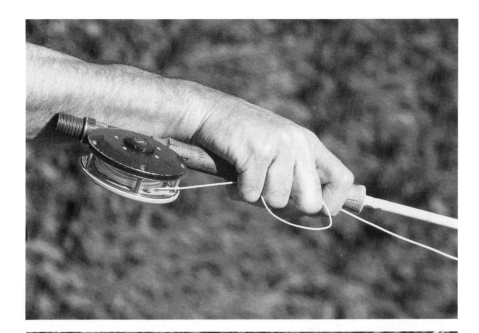

When in a wind blowing from your right to your left, you must put the line and fly to your left, downwind and safe. Start by turning the wrist so that the back of the hand is on top. Now do the cast in the normal way, except that . . .

. . . The right thumb is taken to the left ear instead of to the right ear. This leans the rod well to the left, drives the backcast to the left rear and, however hard the wind blows, you cannot get a fly stuck in you.

Because the cast started with the back of the hand on top, it must finish with the back of the hand on top. The wrist is rolled upright only as the drift down takes place: any earlier, and the cast will go too low and crash hard onto the water.

The American way of putting the backcast on the left. The rod hand stays on the right, but the rod is leaned over the head, so that the tip tracks back and forth on the left-hand side of the angler. Not quite as powerful as the position shown on page 43, but easier for a beginner to learn in his or her early days.

cast is started, the right hand which is holding the rod should be turned on its side, so that the back of the hand is on top. The back of the hand stays on top during the whole of the backcast, and during the push of the forward cast. This is absolutely essential.

There is a greater temptation to cock the wrist back in the extremity of the backcast when casting over the left shoulder. I find it easiest to cure this in students by suggesting that they touch the root of the thumb to their left cheek as they stop the backcast and, providing the butt of the rod is still touching the forearm, as it should be, the rod has stopped at 12.30 and the backcast will go high.

On the forward cast, the back of the right hand must be on top throughout the push. If the wrist is rolled so that the thumb is on top at the completion of the push, the cast will go too low, usually crashing on the water several yards short of the target.

The wrist should be brought back to the vertical (handshake position) only during the drift down, and after the line is long committed to a correct aiming point.

There is, of course, nothing wrong with the method favoured by our American cousins, where the right elbow is stuck out a bit, which leans the rod to the left. The thumb is tracked back over the head, and the result is similar – the line goes to the left, downwind. There is a slight disadvantage in that the muscles which drive the rod forward with the right elbow stuck out to the side are not as powerful as the muscles which drive the rod forward with the right elbow more tucked in, so the UK method of taking the right thumb to the left ear (and no higher than the ear) will yield slightly more distance for less effort on your part.

When double-hauling (see Chapter 8), some people find it easier to use the American style just mentioned, rather than the left-ear style. With a little practice, both are easy, but some people find the coordination of double-hauling requires their rod hand to be on the right-hand side of the head. If this applies to you, adopt the US method of tilting only the rod to the left, keeping the rod hand on the right. As long as the *line and leader and fly* track on your downwind side, and are thus safe against any sudden gust of wind blowing a fly into your face, it matters not how you are happiest achieving the desired result. Remember that it is the track of the rod tip which matters – the *tip ring* must track on your left-hand side, even if it is only a couple of feet off the vertical as it does so.

6
THE OVERHEAD CAST –
Into the Wind

The average angler, facing into the wind, tries to cast by putting more effort into the forward cast. The line goes out and, as it hovers above the surface for a split second, the leader blows back, landing in a heap somewhere around the end of the fly line. In a good stiff wind, the fly sometimes blows so far back that the leader is pointing back at his feet. Seeing this happen, our tyro then puts more effort into the next cast. The leader still blows back before it lands. The third attempt tears his underwear with the huge force applied, and the leader *still* blows back before it lands. The angler then checks his leader and finds that there are a couple of knots in it, usually about a yard from the tail fly. Obviously something is wrong.

Actually, our tyro is lucky that he didn't rise a fish on one of those casts, as a 'wind knot' reduces the strength of the nylon by over 50 per cent, and there was a strong possibility of a ping of breaking tippet as the strike was made.

Wind knots are caused by too much effort, not by the wind. And too much effort is one of the commonest casting faults in windy conditions.

Casting into a wind is easy, once the basic principle is grasped. It requires very little more effort than does casting in still air. All one has to do is to aim lower in front, so that the 'hover' is taken out of the cast, and, as soon as the line and leader are straight, they touch down on the water instead of being blown back.

I say 'aim lower' with some hesitation, as one does *not* aim at a lower point on the push forward. If you drive your thumb out to a lower aiming point it costs you a lower trajectory, and thus it costs you distance. You 'deliver lower' in front by *altering the backcast*, and by doing nothing else different at all!

Let me explain. If you put a higher backcast up there behind you, it will run downhill (forwards) at a steeper angle, and will automatically deliver to a lower landing zone, even if your right thumb tracked outwards to the top of that tree on the horizon. The leader and line will land as soon as they are straight, and the leader will not have time to blow back. Simple, isn't it?

The higher backcast is achieved by lifting the rod point only to 9 o'clock (instead of to 10 o'clock) and flicking only to 12 o'clock (instead of to 12.30). In other words, the power of the backcast is put in earlier, and the rod is stopped earlier. That throws a higher backcast, which will run downhill more steeply, and land out there in front of you as straight as an arrow. Well, I said it was simple, didn't I?

I can hear you saying that it cannot be as simple as that. There must be some other magic ingredient, otherwise you would have been able to do it all by yourself without my telling you. I can assure you that there is nothing else to do except stop that rod tip exactly upright in the backcast, and I mean absolutely vertical. Lots of anglers *think* they are stopping the tip in a vertical position whereas it is coming back to 1 o'clock.

There are occasions when there is a real wind blowing in your face. I mean a Force Eight, a real gale, when sane men would be at home watching football on television, but you, fishing nut that you are, are determined to catch a fish. In conditions like this, a little extra is sometimes needed, and the key to success is a little single-haul on the forward cast in addition to stopping the rod at 12 o'clock. I must stress that the little extra is *never* the application of more force with the rod hand – that is the little extra which contributes wind knots to your other problems, and we all have enough problems without wind knots! (See page 60.)

There has been much pseudo-scientific burble written about casting into

Stopping the rod absolutely vertical – well, nearly so! – in the backcast, so raises the backcast that the forward cast runs downhill at a steeper angle, and goes lower before it lands. Thus the leader will land as soon as it finishes its turnover, and before it can blow back into a heap.

If you normally hover your fly 2 feet or so off the surface before it lands, then raising the extremity of your backcast by 2 feet will take that hover out, and your leader will not blow back. Remember the golden rule for casting into wind – *No more effort by the rod hand.* Fail to appreciate this and you will suffer from wind knots in your leader.

47

the wind. Expressions like 'Cut the line down under the wind', and suggestions that there is less wind down on the surface than there is at the height of the rod tip. There may be less wind at the roots of waist-high bracken than there is at face level, but on a lake I have found that there is damn-all difference in the strength of the wind coming across open water. If there was that much less wind at water level, why are my wellies being filled by those waves? So forget all those glib words about trying to cut the line under the wind – just stop the rod at 12 o'clock in the backcast, and take it easy. You will be amazed at how simple it is.

If you ever find yourself trying to cast into a lake where the tops of the waves are being blown off by the wind, and little waterspouts are chasing each other, I suggest you look for a sheltered bay where insects might be blown off the trees on to the water and, if it is in the latter part of the season, a daddy-long-legs might do great execution. Or go home and watch football. I confess that I have seen a few days when any sort of fly fishing proved impossible – on one occasion my line was picked off the surface and held vertically above my head for a full minute. All I could do was to roar with laughter and tell myself I was a fool for being there!

7

THE OVERHEAD CAST – Casting a Little Farther

Most fly rods are marked with an AFTM number. This is designed by the rod builder to give you a guide to the weight of line which should be hung outside the rod tip. For instance, if the rod says AFTM 7, it is intended to tell you that the correct weight is *10 yards* of No. 7 line outside the tip ring. Plus the little level tip on the line, plus leader, of course. If you hang more line, and thus a greater weight, outside the tip ring, the spring of the rod will become soggy, and you will lose crispness and tip speed. If you lose tip speed you lose line speed. Line speed is what gives you distance.

It follows therefore that it is a mistake to hang too much line outside the tip ring. It is called 'aerialising' by the cognoscenti. Aerialise more than 10 yards and you overload the rod. It may not break, as it will usually have a great reserve of strength, but you will lose tip speed unless you put more effort into your casting. Carried to its logical conclusion, one sees some reservoir anglers doing strenuous gymnastics under their fly rods just to keep a vast amount of line in the air before they finally deliver it out into the blue yonder. There is an easy way, which takes a lot less out of you. It is called 'shooting line'.

There are many forms of shooting a line. One example was when I heard three anglers in a Montana bar talking about the merits of their fishing boats:

'My boat will float in one inch of water'.
'My boat will float on wet grass.'
'My boat will float where water *was*'.

That was the ultimate line shoot, and not at all uncommon amongst anglers in a bar, but we are now going to discuss shooting fly lines, not verbal ones.

Start by assuming you have just done the simple overhead cast which we have already discussed, that there is no wind, and yet you want to cast farther. Pull 4 or 5 yards of fly line off the reel. Trap the line again under your little finger of the right hand, and grasp the line firmly in the left hand. While you have line lying at your feet, keep your feet still – commandment number one says 'Thou shalt not stand on your own flyline'. Stand on somebody else's line if you are spoiling for a fight, but never your own.

Now do an overhead cast, exactly the same as we have just been doing,

If you are shooting only a yard or so of line, keep it trapped under the right forefinger during the cast, and when the rod stops, simply straighten the forefinger and the line will shoot. This applies also to double-handed rods, as in this photograph.

but aim a little higher on the forward push. (Imagine the water on the landing zone is a yard deeper than it really is.) At the very moment the rod stops at the end of the push, let the line go from your left hand. The loose line will zip out through the rings, and the whole line will hover and land gently, with the fly 4 or 5 yards further away than before.

Remember you have aerialised only 10 yards of line. You have used the momentum given to that 10 yards to pull another 4 yards out after it. Do not think you have now cast only 14 yards – you have 3 yards of rod, and 3 yards (at least) of leader, so the fly should have landed 20 yards from your toes. What you have achieved is a 20-yard cast, using only the energy needed to throw 10 yards of line, and that is an economy of effort which will allow you to keep fishing all day instead of sleeping in the afternoon!

It is absolutely vital that you do not let the line in the left hand slip at all. Any slippage here will take all the power out of either the backcast or the forward cast. Equally it is vital that you dump the line altogether from the left hand when the rod stops. If you merely slacken your grip and let the line run over the palm of your hand you will be adding friction which will prevent some of the shoot. If you form an 'O' with the thumb and forefinger of the left hand (advised by some to guide the line into the butt ring), you will add friction. That line is going to go out through the butt ring because it is being pulled from the far side of the butt ring by the line already in the air, so there is no need whatever to guide it. Just dump it altogether and it will shoot as far as possible.

As soon as the line lands, grab the line with the left hand and hook it over the forefinger of the right hand. You can now pull the fly towards you by pulling inboard of your right forefinger. No reaching up to the butt ring every pull, as is done by those who have the line trapped by only the middle finger of the rod hand. Pull in inboard of the forefinger, save effort. You also feel takes on the pad of the forefinger, which is quite sensitive.

To shoot more line, the slack should be held in the left hand, and when the rod stops, dump the line altogether. Do not merely slacken the grip and let the line run over the palm – this adds friction and will cost you distance. For the same reason, do not form an 'O' with finger and thumb to guide the line. It does not need guiding, as all the momentum is coming from the line already outside the tip ring, and this pulls slack into and through the butt ring without any assistance from you.

You now have say 14 yards of line outside the tip ring, and can work the fly towards you by pulling line in over the right forefinger. When you have retrieved as much line as you want to, and are ready to cast again, take the line off the right forefinger with the left hand and go through the same cast again. If you have 10 yards of line to aerialise, you will not need any false casting – once back into a nice high backcast, and deliver and shoot. If you have less than 10 yards to aerialise you might have to do one false cast, shooting a little line either into the backcast or into the forward cast, or into both, but there is no need for much thrashing around. False casting just burns up your breakfast and should be avoided whenever possible.

If you wish, then once you have your 14 yards of line lying out there on the surface in front of you, you can try another 4 yards off the reel, aerialise the 14 yards, shoot another 4 or 5, and you are now casting perhaps 25 yards. With only one backcast . . . .

It may well be that your rod does not feel happy with that weight on the tip. You will also realise that the backcast pause takes a little longer, as there is more line to flow out straight behind you. What you should realise also is that you should use *no more effort* – just give the line a slightly higher trajectory, and it will all go, believe me.

If you wish to fire a rifle bullet farther, you merely cock the barrel up a bit. You do not drive the bullet faster, as the power is contained in the cartridge case to a fixed degree and cannot be altered. But a higher trajectory will allow the bullet to go farther before it hits the ground. It is just the same with a fly line – aim higher and it will go farther before it hits the water.

Of course I realise that casting a line farther does take more effort. This is an immutable law of physics. But the average angler puts too much effort into short casts, and if he puts the same effort into longer casts they will in all probability go out nicely. I have found it easiest to teach people to cast farther by telling them – '*no more effort*'. (Equally my commonest comment to an angler with some fishing experience behind him is to tell him '*less effort*'). It is an enlightening experience for the average angler to see just how little effort it takes to throw a nice line when the mechanics of the cast are executed well.

Having aerialised 14 yards of fly line, and shot perhaps another 5, there is still some line wound on the reel. How much depends on the line manufacturer. Some lines are still sold as 30 yards long for a double-taper, or 35 yards for a weight-forward. Many makes are nowadays selling lines in a standard 25-metre (about 27 yards) length. There are several reasons for this. The average angler never sees that last few yards come off the reel in the life of the line, so why sell him more line than he will ever need? There is also the psychological factor that an angler who casts the whole of the fly line out will think that he is wielding a smashing fly rod, and that the line is a beauty, well worth what he paid for it! He may well get a boost to his ego when he realises that he 'has cast the whole fly line out'. Never having actually measured it, he thinks it is 30 yards, and who is going to spoil things by telling him that it is only 27? It was still a cast enjoyed by fewer than 50 per cent of anglers, I can assure you.

I must stress that there is one vital thing about shooting line. It is impera-

tive that you do not let the line go until the rod stops. I have read articles on casting which suggest that it is correct to shoot the line 'at the moment of maximum power' – do that and the line will land in a heap, far short of the target. You dump the line at the moment you have *finished applying maximum power*. By doing this you utilise the impetus you have already given to the aerialised line to drag the rest out after it.

If you let go too soon, the certain symptom is that the line will wrap around the blank between the cork handle and the butt ring. If you let go too late, the line will not shoot, and you will be left with some slack hanging on the near side of the butt ring. If the line shoots, and then makes a 'slap' noise against the rod, you put too much effort into the cast. You also put too much effort into the cast, and you were not holding the line trapped under the little finger, if the reel ratchet makes a noise as all the line stops out in front of you. (It may well kick back if you put too much effort into the cast, and that costs you distance.)

Shooting line is easy if you put into it only the amount of effort required, and let the line go the instant the *rod stops after the push*.

If you try to shoot the line by letting go before the rod stops, the line will wrap around the blank like this.

Shooting line with a weight-forward fly line becomes very much more difficult if you have too much line out, so that more than a yard of the thin running line is outside the tip ring. Very good, well-coordinated casters can manage perhaps 3 yards of 'overhang' (the thin running line behind the back taper of a weight-forward or shooting head), but as a general rule the rod is not capable of transmitting power smoothly through too much thin line to that thick chunk beyond it.

One of the best tips for a beginner is to suggest that he threads a weight-forward line onto his rod, measures the amount of line he can comfortably aerialise, and marks the point where the left hand will grip the line. A black felt pen works quite well on light-coloured lines. Each cast can then be made with the correct amount of line out for good control and maximum distance of shoot.

Let us now consider how to cast the whole fly line out.

8
THE OVERHEAD CAST –
Casting a Lot Farther

Watching anglers around our reservoirs, I am struck by the amount of effort expended by the average man, and by the limited distance achieved. I think it would be true to say that a cast of over 25 yards is achieved by fewer than 50 per cent of anglers, and a cast of over 30 yards by fewer than 10 per cent of anglers. Perhaps 5 per cent of anglers can ever reach over 35 yards – and that 5 per cent will be well-coordinated and well-taught. It is also probably true to say that the 10 per cent of anglers who can cast over 30 yards form the 10 per cent of anglers, quoted by Richard Walker, who catch 90 per cent of the fish.

Not that sheer distance is essential to the catching of lots of fish. Remember that the most important distance in trout fishing is the 6 inches between your ears, and using that distance constructively will put more fish in the bag than hurling fly lines out to incredible distances. But there will be occasions when the number of fish caught will be in direct proportion to the distance cast. These occasions will perhaps be in early spring, when the colour of lure for the day, and the depth at which to strip it back, become well known along a shore full of anglers, and one's catch will be in proportion to the number of fish which see one's fly. It is a mathematical certainty that the farther one casts, the larger the area of water covered, and the more trout will see the fly.

Distance casting is most efficiently done with a shooting head, although a weight-forward line is next best, and a double-taper the least efficient. The efficiency is in proportion to the friction through the rod rings on the shoot. A double-taper line is thick, has most friction through the rings, and will shoot least. A weight-forward line is thinner through the rings and will shoot farther than will a double-taper. A shooting head, backed by some form of thin running line, has least friction and will shoot farthest. I say 'some form' of running line deliberately, as different people have different preferences for the material from which the running line is made.

Fine nylon monofilament has least friction, but tends to tangle. Nylon monofilament which has been partly flattened into an oval section also has very little friction, and tends to tangle less. Braided monofilament has a bit more friction, but tangles still less, and has a nicer feel in the left hand. Very fine dressed fly line has more friction, tangles least, and has the sort of feel to which we have become accustomed – but now we are almost back to a weight-forward, as that is basically only a shooting head with fine dressed line behind it. (But without the knot joining the two!) Whatever kind of running line you choose, it will tangle from time to time, and I have never found the complete answer to this.

There is one item of kit which you might find useful if you are going to use a shooting head for much of your fishing, and that is some form of container for the line after it has been stripped in. Line trays are one alternative, and they can be designed to strap around the waist or low on the left hip. I have always found them cumbersome. I have seen line trays designed to float beside the left leg, and these are often larger than the ones which strap to one's person. I have also seen plastic buckets, washing-up bowls, and various other receptacles used to strip the line into, and, while the man at Rutland with a red washing-up bowl strapped to his left hip was perhaps fishing very efficiently, he was not exactly a model of sartorial elegance. But who cares what one's fishing outfit looks like? Nowadays I dump my running line on to the bank beside me, trying for a clear space without thistles to tangle in, or into the water beside my feet and putting up with the slight lack of distance caused by the friction of the line having sunk in coils.

How long should a shooting head be? This is a question I am often asked – and how long is a piece of string? The only practical answer is that your shooting head should balance your rod and your casting style, and should be tailor-made for that rod. Here is how to do it.

As most shooting-head work is done with a sinker, buy yourself a double-tapered sinking line one AFTM number higher than the maker's rating for the rod. If the rod is rated No. 7, buy yourself a DT 8. Thread the line through the rod rings, leaving the bulk of the line on the ground at your feet. Tie on a length of heavy nylon to act as a temporary leader. Now do some false casting, letting a little line out through the rings from time to time, until you reckon that the amount of line you are aerialising feels right. Too much and the rod will feel soggy. Too little and you will feel that you could lift more. When it is just right, you will feel that the line is travelling nice and fast through the air, and the rod still feels crisp. Now lay the rod down on the ground and walk to the tip ring. Cut the line 1 foot outside the tip ring. The piece of line lying out towards your target is now your shooting head for that rod.

You can sell the rest of the double-taper line to a friend so that he can make himself a shooting head with the other end of the double-taper. The bit left from the centre of the line can be used to tie up the roses, unless you are also a salmon angler, in which case you can make some sink-tips out of it for attachment to a floating salmon line. (Lengths of DT 8 will match very well a DT 10, 11 or 12 salmon line to give a sink-tip line which does not suffer from the feeling that the line has a brick tied to the end of it, as so many factory sink-tips do!)

Back to your shooting head, lying on the grass. Strip a little of the butt end (where you cut it) to remove the plastic dressing and expose the core. Make a loop in the core, either by simply knotting it or, neater, by whipping a loop and varnishing the whipping. To this loop you tie your running line, whether it be monofilament or braid, and you have a shooting head outfit which balances your rod and personal casting style.

Double-hauling. Start with the rod tip low, and no slack under the tip ring; with rod held in the right hand, line in the left hand, and hands together. (For a greater length of haul you can, if you wish, reach the left hand forward and grasp the line near the butt ring, but this involves much more effort – see the illustrations for competition casting in Chapter 9.)

Raise the rod slowly to 10 o'clock, hands still together. This movement slides the line on the water towards you and breaks the surface tension. You are now ready to start the flick upwards and backwards, and to start hauling with the left hand.

The backcast flick completed, the left-hand haul completed. Notice that the rod has come farther back than in an ordinary overhead cast as the 'stride is lengthened', but that the line is still heading backwards in an upwards direction for a high flowing backcast. As soon as the rod stops here, the left hand starts coming back to the right ear.

While the backcast is flowing out, the left hand moves smoothly back to the right ear, feeding the line under control to the butt ring. Do not hurry this movement – if you do, slack line will develop inboard of the butt ring and you will lose the smooth flow of the backcast. Note how the line near the tip has started to drop – the reason for putting it high in the first place.

As soon as the line is all straight behind, the forward thrust of the rod is started, and the left hand starts to haul downwards. Here the forward cast is well under way.

The forward drive of the rod is now completed, and the rod is stopping. The left-hand haul is completed and, at this moment, the left hand will release the line for the shoot. Note the long thrust of the right thumb, out to full arm-stretch in front, in order to deliver that forward power over as long a time-span as possible.

Note that, in this series of photographs, the angler is standing relaxed, and no apparent effort is being used. If your casting looks to others as if you are doing callisthenics, you will not be able to fish for long without rest.

Remember the old carpenter's motto when you are approaching the line to cut it – you can always cut more off, but you cannot put it back. Test whether the head is right for you before you go fishing with it, as there is no point in wasting fishing time in rectifying a mistake which should have been discovered at home. And you did remember to put the reel on the rod before you waved it around, didn't you? Leave the reel off, and the rod will feel much heavier than it should, due to the lack of a counterbalance weight behind the hand.

It should be realised that the critical thing about a shooting head is its *weight*. Length is immaterial, providing you can keep it aerialised. Looking at the AFTM scale, 10 yards of No. 8 line weights 210 grains. This is the same weight as:

$$15 \text{ yards AFTM } 5$$
$$13\tfrac{1}{8} \text{ yards AFTM } 6$$
$$11\tfrac{1}{3} \text{ yards AFTM } 7$$
$$10 \text{ yards AFTM } 8$$
$$8\tfrac{3}{4} \text{ yards AFTM } 9$$
$$7\tfrac{1}{2} \text{ yards AFTM } 10$$
$$6\tfrac{1}{3} \text{ yards AFTM } 11.$$

Remember also that the thinner a fly line the less wind resistance it has, and the farther it will go before wind resistance stops it. In theory therefore a shooting head made of 15 yards of AFTM 5 will go farther than a head made of 10 yards of AFTM 8 – providing you can aerialise 15 yards of head. This was the theory behind the Masterline Banker, basically a long shooting head of thinner line, the total weight of which would not overload a rod rated 8 or 9. A superb line, it did not achieve the success it deserved, as too few average anglers could keep such a long head in the air. Good casters fell in love with it, however. Having got the basic kit of rod, reel, running line and shooting head, with a length of nylon as a leader, we can start to consider how to cast a long way. We use a technique called double-hauling.

Double-hauling is the name given to a casting style where the line is made to move faster through the air than the spring of the rod by itself is capable of doing. The extra speed is given to the line by pulling with the left hand while the rod is bent, both in the backcast and the forward cast. If you pull on only one of the rod movements, it is called single-hauling. The double-haul involves a pull in both directions, and requires a degree of coordination which many anglers find difficult to master. I will come back to this pull in a moment. First let us consider whether the right hand, the one holding and driving the rod, does anything different.

When it comes to the difference between the normal overhead cast and double-hauling, there is an almost exact parallel in the difference between walking and running. So far we have talked about walking when we discussed the ordinary overhead cast, and the act of shooting line. Double-hauling is the equivalent of running. To change from a walk to a run, a human being lengthens the stride and puts a little more effort into the legs. To change from 'normal' casting to double-hauling, one lengthens the stride of the rod arm, and of the rod itself, and puts a little more effort into both the backwards flick and into the forward push. The lengthening of the stride involves starting the flick earlier, stopping the flick still around 12.30, but then drifting backwards with the rod tip to perhaps 2 o'clock, so that the forward push can go all the way from 2 o'clock right out to full arm-stretch in front. So both the backcast and the forward cast have the power built into them over a longer stroke – just like lengthening the stride when running. The amount of *extra effort* is up to you – unless you are intent upon casting out of sight it requires very *little extra effort* – all it needs is power applied over a longer time – that is more total power than before, but at any one moment you will be expending very *little extra effort*. This is the reason why the very good caster makes it look effortless, and why the good caster can keep fishing for a long time after the poor caster has collapsed into a heap of jellified muscle! The commonest mistake for the beginner is to try too hard with that right arm, and the symptom will be the appearance of wind knots in the leader.

It is the coordination of the work done by the left hand which causes most problems to the beginner. It is easy enough to start with the hands close together in front of the body, right hand holding the rod, left hand holding the line, and, as the rod starts the flick backwards, the left hand pulls the line down through the butt ring. Then the end of the backcast is reached, and the right hand has stopped around the right ear. The left hand *must now be taken up to the right ear*, so that both hands are again together, ready for the right hand to push forward, and the left hand to haul again.

I used to teach double-hauling by telling the student the following:

Hands together. Both hands are held with knuckles touching, low in front of the body, right hand on the rod, left hand on the line.
Hands apart. The right hand tracks back to the right ear, the left hand goes leftwards and downwards to pull line down through the rings as the rod tracks back.
Hands together. The right hand stays still beside the ear. The left hand comes up and back, still holding the line, until the hands are again together beside the right ear. During this movement the line is flowing out behind in the backcast – there is plenty of time for the hand to come up and back smoothly, so that the line stays tight and under control inboard of the butt ring.
Hands apart. The right hand thrusts out to full arm-stretch in the forward push. The left hand again pulls line downwards and leftwards, with the left hand ending up beside the left waist. As soon as the rod stops, the left hand releases line to shoot.

That was the theory. Teaching somebody to do it was a different matter altogether. The hard part was getting the student to get that hand back to the ear before the forward cast started, and the result was often a haul on the backcast, followed by a release of line on the forward cast, Not the idea at all, and it took all the power out of the forward delivery. One student suggested that it was a 'scissor action', or so he had read, and he had been told that the movement of the arms was like the opening and closing of the blades of a pair of scissors. I tried this analogy on a few students, and they ended up more confused than before. Finally I found that the best way was not to explain anything, but to tell the student to do the casting with his right hand, while I grasped his left hand and the line and moved it for him. After a few false casts I was able to let go and leave him to do the left hand movements on his own. Simple. But then I was asked over the telephone how it was done, and it was no good my saying that I grab your hand and do it for you!

Some years ago I watched a video tape made by an American instructor, Mel Krieger. With a lovely infectious grin, Mel showed the easy way of teaching the double-haul, and I have used his method ever since. Mel says, 'You learn a new word. It is one word, not two. The word is *downup*. As the rod moves, you look at your left hand and say *downup*. On the forward cast you say *downup* again'. It is so blindingly simple, easy to explain, easy to follow, that it is a prime example of 'Why didn't I think of that?' By following this method of talking to the left hand, and perhaps accentuating the second syllable so that it sounds like 'down*up*', the left hand gets the message and tracks back to the ear before the start of the forward haul. Eureka, as the man said. Using this method I have cut by about 50 per cent the time it takes to teach the double-haul, from perhaps 15 minutes to less than 10, always assuming that the student can cast a reasonable line without any hauling. Thank you, Mel.

Like patting yourself on the head at the same time as rubbing the tummy, double-hauling requires a certain amount of coordination. Some people are totally uncoordinated. If you walk into every second lamp-post you will take longer to learn to double-haul, but once it has been grooved into your subconscious you will find it easy from then on.

The movement of the left hand must be smooth. If the left hand is jerked, the result will not be a speeding up of the line but a collapse of the spring of the rod. If the rod is thus made to bend past its most powerful point, the line will go slower through the air, not faster. Jerky hauling also causes tailing loops and wind knots.

It is not necessary, in normal fishing conditions, to haul the left hand in great long pulls. If I start with both hands together in front of my waist and take my left hand *1 foot* leftwards and downwards, at the same time as my right hand has tracked up to beside my right ear, I have actually pulled *3 feet* of line down through the butt ring, and that is plenty. The problem is that my left hand then has to move that *3 feet* up to my right ear before I can start the forward cast, and that is what takes the coordination. On the forward cast my left hand travels *3 feet* from beside my right ear to that lowest position beside my left thigh. I think that the reservoir angler suffers a lot of problems as a result of seeing photographs of competition anglers at play. A few years ago I saw an advertisement for a brand of fishing rod picturing a man in an exquisite ballet-dancing pose, leaning right back from the toes, arms far behind him. It was supposed to suggest that he was using a super fishing rod, but all it conveyed to me was that he would not last long if he had to cast like that all day! Good double-hauling should be a totally relaxed activity, using very little more energy than normal casting, but throwing the line perhaps 20 per cent farther. I would suggest that, if you cast between 20 and 25 yards merely by shooting line, you should aim for 25 to 30 yards by double-hauling. If you try constantly to cast 40 yards you will not last the day, and fishing will become just another gymnastic exercise, where only the trained athlete can succeed.

Timing is all important, particularly timing the forward cast. It does help if you watch the backcast rolling out, and for this a sideways stance is vital. Put your left foot forward, turn your shoulders so that the left shoulder leads at the target, and you can then turn your head to watch the backcast without your arm swinging out sideways. When the timing is grooved into your subconscious you can stand facing your target, totally relaxed, and double-haul happily away. If you watch the backcast all the time, you will end a fishing day with 'tennis neck'. If, of course, there is a high bank or obstruction behind, you should watch to make sure that the fly is not going to catch on anything – it is a recipe for a sickening crack and a shower of black bits around your ears to hook the fly on a barbed wire fence just as you start to deliver a great powerful forward cast.

Which brings me to the need for no more power on that final delivery. By all means shoot a little line on each false cast. Beware the total amount of 'overhang' you develop outside the tip ring – too much and the whole lot lands in a heap as you lose control of the line in the air. Once the line is flowing back and forth sweetly, do *not* say to yourself 'Next time' and give a great drive of the rod to deliver the line out of sight over the far horizon. It will not go nearly as far as if you saw the line flowing sweetly and, *without any more effort*, just let it sail out. Remember the need for a high trajectory, aim high, and just let it sail away, letting go with the left hand just at the moment the haul finishes and the rod tip stops.

For the average angler, merely wanting to cast a reasonable distance with the amount of effort he can sustain all day, my advice would be to get 1–2 yards of overhang, get the line moving with only *one* false cast, and then let it fly out over the water. False casting achieves one very definite result – it makes you feel warmer! It also frightens fish if you flicker a wet fly line over their heads (and a wet fly line will flash in the sun whatever its colour). So do yourself a favour and cut down that false casting – you will live longer. If you get it right at the back the first time, you need only that one backcast, and can let the cast fly out. You will not improve things by doing three false casts, although I did see one man at Rutland doing seventeen false casts before he delivered his fly on to empty water in front of him – I counted them in total fascination.

Competition casting is not fishing. It started out many years ago as a derivative of fishing, and it is true to say that good competition casters are usually good anglers, but to emulate the competition caster while fishing is rather like trying to commute to work in traffic while driving a Formula One racing car. A distance competition consists of a man standing on a platform for 7 minutes. He may cast as often as he wishes in that 7 minutes, and the best two casts count for score. At the end of 7 minutes he comes off that platform with wobbly knees, sweat running down his purple face, and his arms all one big hurt. There is no point on the hook, so if the fly touches the grass behind it does not matter; in fact it can be a benefit as the extra resistance tends to cock the spring of the rod for a more powerful delivery. Between each cast he has to pull in all the running line, laying it in a zigzag pattern so that it does not tangle on the next shoot, rather as the coastguards do with a rocket line, and this, of course, is done in a hurry, bent double, and with both hands. At the average British casting competition, whether at club or international level, one will not even be in the prize list unless one can cast well over 60 yards, and it has become a young, fit, man's game. Having said that, the techniques developed over the years at casting competitions have benefited the materials and design of fishing tackle to an incredible degree, the men and women who take part are friendly and most hospitable, and you would be welcomed with open arms if you went to a casting competition with the announced intention of trying to learn something.

But do not confuse competition casting with fishing. One is an endurance test for 7 minutes, the other you will want to do all day.

Quite the most economical style of double-hauling I have ever seen is that done by Donald Downs. As this is written, Donald is around 70 years of age. His left hand hauls for only a few inches – just a tiny tug on the line. His timing, of course, is impeccable, his stance is totally relaxed, and the line flows out to distances greater than those achieved by almost any reservoir angler, and yet there is no apparent effort, just that tiny pull of a few inches, done somewhere in front of his chin, under that wonderful moustache! The message in this paragraph is that you should not feel that double-hauling necessarily involves a great heave with the left hand – just enough pull to speed the line up a little is all that is really required. Put into each cast only the amount of energy you think you can sustain for the whole of an 8-hour fishing day.

9
THE OVERHEAD CAST –
The Ultimate in Distance

This is not a chapter telling you how to cast while fishing. It is intended to be a description of how competition casters belt lines out to incredible distances, and if there is anything in this chapter which you feel you can adopt in your fishing, and your muscles will withstand the strain, then so be it.

In 1931, the year I was born, the world record fly cast stood at something like 41 yards. Double-hauling was developed soon after that, and the record jumped to about 60 yards. Currently the world record (and I confess that I may not be quite up-to-date) stands at about 80 yards. I have already said that competition casting bears little resemblance to the kind of casting you can maintain for the whole of a long fishing day, but an understanding of the technique might one day help you to reach that distant fish. Please do not think that these great distances are attained with normal fishing tackle; they are not. A competition trout fly rod is a beast, and few men have the muscles to wield it. With a normal fly rod and shooting head, anybody who can cast over 45 yards is one of the chosen few, I can assure you. British Game Fair competitions are regularly won with lesser distances than this.

The competition distance caster nowadays is an athlete. The ones who win in international competitions tend to be employed by rod makers, who have a vested interest in their products being seen to perform. Hours and hours of practice are required, keeping the muscles and the timing constantly honed to peak performance. Hours and hours nowadays are spent casting in front of a video camera, so that the slightest modification to muscular movement and timing can be analysed and studied. I am not a competition caster. I attended a couple of meetings of the British Casting Association when I was in my mid-40s, and quickly realised that these nice men I met there were totally dedicated, fitter than I felt, and were happy to spend long hours, often long lonely hours, on a sports field somewhere, belting a line out and pacing the result time after time until it got too dark to see! It was not my scene. I listened to their talk of overhang, test curves, grams weight of line, and I learned a great deal from them, but I could not bring myself to give the necessary dedication to just casting as far as I could. It was, however, an essential part of my education as a casting instructor just to watch the incredible results they achieved, and to study how they did it.

To cast a fly line, preferably a shooting head, as far as possible with the

Double-hauling for sheer distance. Reaching forward, left leg well bent, line grasped in the left hand as far forward as possible.

The lift completed, left hand starting the haul, rod slightly flexed under the influence of the straightened left leg.

Backwards flick well under way, haul well in progress, body starting to rock backwards.

Shoulders starting to turn, right leg starting to bend.

tackle you have, imitate the competition caster. Your tackle will be quite different but the casting style is that which will cast farthest with any tackle. An apt analogy is handing your standard saloon car to a trained racing driver. He will use every inch of the circuit, toe-and-heel gear changes, cadence braking, and will take your car round the circuit at speeds which would terrify a normal driver, and do so in safety. Try to emulate him without the training, and you will overcook it on the first corner and turn the car into a heap of scrap metal. If you want to get the maximum performance out of standard fishing tackle, use the techniques of the competition caster.

Stand sideways to your target, left shoulder leading, and feet well apart. Start with the right elbow bent, but the left hand reaching out far in front of you to the butt ring, where the line is gripped. The line you are going to aerialise is all laid out straight in front of you, with no slack under the tip ring. Now bend your left knee and reach forward as far as you can, changing the left-hand grip to remove the little bit of slack which appeared as you leaned forward. You are now standing like a cocked spring, ready for the backcast.

Remember line speed is vital. So the power of the backcast is composed of three parts. Firstly, the almost normal, but very powerful, lift and flick

Haul completed, power coming off the rod. The line has been driven backwards, over the tip of the rod, to allow plenty of time for lining up the forward cast while the line drops at the extremity of the backcast.

Backcast now completed as the drift of the right hand stops. Left hand starts to feed line backwards under control towards the butt ring.

The moment of starting the forward cast. The right leg is now well bent, the rod is at full stride, the forward haul about to start.

The rod is pulled in towards the ball of the shoulder, the haul is starting, the right leg has thrust forwards, bending the left knee, shoulders starting to turn and thrust towards the target.

The whole weight of the body is now behind the rod, right hand in a powerful punching position, haul well under way, and the right thumb under pressure.

The right arm has punched out, thumb pressing hard on the handle to turn the rod towards the final angle of delivery, haul nearly completed.

Haul completed, and line released by the left hand. Right leg has finished its forward thrust. The rod is pointing along the direction of flight of the line as it shoots through the rings.

It will be readily seen that casting for maximum distance bears more resemblance to a mixture of ballet dancing and gymnastics than it does to the gentle art of angling. However, an understanding of the techniques involved in casting like this may help on the rare occasions when you really do want to cast out into the blue yonder for that tantalising giant trout.

with the right hand and arm. Secondly the long haul with the left hand, starting at a point well out in front beside the butt ring, and ending up at full arm-stretch downwards and to the left. Thirdly the thrust of the left thigh muscles, shifting the whole weight of the body backwards, compressing the right thigh muscles, and thus moving the shoulders rearwards by perhaps 4 feet.

The pause has more to it than a normal cast. While the line is flying backwards, unrolling in a tight loop, the right hand is drifted backwards to full arm-stretch at about shoulder height. The left hand also drifts back, feeding line under control through the rings, so that the left arm is also stretched out rearwards. At the extremity of the backcast, therefore, one is ready for as long a forward delivery as possible – remember that power applied over a longer time is more total power.

When the brain triggers the start of the forward cast, the first thing which happens is an inwards draw of the right hand towards the right shoulder. The left hand then starts the haul, and the right thigh thrusts the whole body to the left, towards the target. As the right hand reaches the area of the right ear, it continues as powerfully as possible, thrusting the right thumb out, high above the target. The left hand hauls as far as possible, ending up at full arm-stretch somewhere behind the left thigh. At the same time as all this is going on, there is a sharp turn from the waist to bring the shoulders round to face square on to the target, so that the right shoulder is made to travel towards the target, reinforcing the thrust of the right arm muscles.

The idea is to get a low backcast, kissing the fly (which has no point or barb on it) on the ground or water at the extremity of the backcast. The little increased drag which this yields will tend to cock the spring of the rod more, thus giving greater speed and distance forwards. With a low backcast, it is easier to throw a high forward cast, with as high a trajectory as possible, with the effort forwards exactly 180° to the backcast.

When the forward thrust is completed, the rod is frozen, pointing along that high forward trajectory, so that the line can shoot out through the rings with as little friction as possible. (Any angle between the rod and line will cause friction at the tip ring.) The caster is frozen, looking rather like a poised ballet dancer, until the line finally lands.

As soon as the fly lands, the caster drops the rod on the platform, and, staring at the judges, bends down to pull the line in through the butt ring, using both hands in a pulley-hauley fashion. The second he sees one of the judge's arms raised to signify that the measurement is registered, the pulling begins, laying the line out in a series of zigzags on the platform to his left. As soon as only a few feet of overhang remain outside the tip ring, he dives for the butt of the rod and the Herculean effort starts all over again. Normally the best two casts in 7 minutes are the only ones to count towards a score.

And if you reckon you can fish like that all day, you are a better man than I am, Gunga Din . . . .

10

THE OVERHEAD CAST –
Faults and Their Cure

Much of what I shall say in this chapter has already been said, but it will be a handy reference for those who have read the book, gone out and tried some casting practice, and found that they have a fault, the cause of which they cannot deduce. I do not claim that this chapter covers *every* fault, as there is bound to be a fault I have not seen, even in my years of teaching and studying the black art of fly casting. Casting is an art, the study of a lifetime, in which you can exhaust yourself but never your subject!

Not in any particular order, these faults can be seen any day around our major reservoirs. Almost inevitably the bearer of the fault thinks that the cure is to apply more effort. Almost inevitably, that solution is wrong, will make the problem worse, and will exhaust the bearer if it is applied.

FLIES CRACK OFF

This fault occurs almost always in the backcast, not the forward cast, and can have two basic causes. Either the backcast is not powerful enough or the timing is wrong. If the backcast does not extend the line fully to the rear, the line will not be straight at the start of the forward thrust. If the backcast is still in a U-shape (the U lying on its side, of course), when one leg of the U is driven forward, the other leg of the U will whip around the bend very fast. The fly, up to that split second travelling backwards, suddenly finds its direction reversed. At the moment of reversal, the fly can exceed the speed of sound – 720 miles an hour – and the crack it makes is symptomatic of the breaking of the sound barrier! Fine nylon cannot stand the terrific jerk of even a size 14 fly changing direction like this, and it will break, with the fly landing in the next county. Subsequent casts will all make a crack noise, telling you that there is no fly on the end of the nylon. Stop and check at the sound of the first crack, or you will find yourself there only for the exercise – you are certainly not going to catch anything if there is no fly on that leader.

If you turn your head to watch the backcast (after turning sideways, left foot forward, of course), you will see whether the fault is caused by insufficient flick backwards, in which case you get the urge to start the forward cast in time to prevent the cast dropping too low, or whether it is caused by simply hurrying the timing by driving the forward cast out before the backcast has had time to straighten. It is easily cured.

BROKEN HOOKS

Fish are frequently blamed for breaking hooks. In my humble experience, I have only once seen a hook broken by a fish, and that was a salmon which crushed a treble flat. I have been present when a salmon broke one of the points of a double hook, and the post mortem decided that one point had entered the top jaw, the other point had stuck in the lower jaw, and the hook had broken when the fish forced its mouth open. Luckily one point stayed in the fish, and the fish was landed. But trout almost never break hooks.

The angler striking at the rise of a trout, feeling a momentary tightening of the line, then everything going slack, looks at the broken hook and says that Brand X hooks are rubbish and he will never buy another! Truth to tell the hook was broken on a previous backcast, and the fish rose to a fly without a point on it.

Low backcasts break hooks. You can sometimes see a stone grow out of the grass and reach up for the point of a hook. As soon as the fly has flicked on the stone and the point has broken off, you will see the stone relax back into the grass! Your fly should never have been anywhere near the grass in the first place – it should have been at least as high above the ground as the point of the rod.

Broken hooks are suffered by men who cock the wrist back during the backcast, bringing the rod too far back and throwing the line low. Or by people who, powerfully muscled, bring the backcast flick back so hard

Cocking the wrist, even only a trifle too far like this, throws the backcast downwards. This fly is actually touching the water at the left of the picture. The shock waves can be seen in the line.

71

that, when they stop the butt of the rod at 12.30, the tip flicks down and back before it recovers and settles also at 12.30. This tip-flick throws the line down behind, instead of it flowing out higher than the rod tip. This man will also suffer from cramp in the forearm after a while, as he is gripping too hard for nice casting. If your knuckles are white, you are gripping too hard. Timing – allowing the backcast too long behind, so that it has time to drop before being driven forward – can also be a cause of broken hooks.

Where fishing is allowed from the dam, and you are short of a fly, take a walk along the top of the dam, or along the roadway which runs along the dam. You will find lots of flies lying on the ground – most of them will have broken hooks, but some of them will merely have been broken off the leader by being smashed against the concrete. Fill your flybox, and reflect how lucky you are that all those anglers did not know how to roll cast, but persisted in doing an overhead cast in a situation where there was insufficient room for a backcast!

LINE LANDS IN A WIGGLE

Basically, a line which lands in a wiggle, and not dead straight, has usually been aimed too high in front, because the backcast was too low. A low backcast *always* causes a wiggle in the forward cast. *Always.*

When I am teaching a beginner, one of the commonest things I am heard to say is 'Low backcast – wiggle, wiggle', and the beginner sees the line, or the leader, land in front of him with a wiggle in it. The wiggle has nothing whatever to do with the forward cast – it is the low backcast which causes the line to climb up over the top of the rod in the forward delivery, aiming automatically too high in front, where it may well be straight while it is 10 feet above the water, but by the time it has fallen to the surface it will have that tell-tale wiggle in it.

Get that backcast up higher by a) not cocking the wrist back, or b) stopping the rod earlier in the backcast (such as 12.30 instead of 1.30), or c) bringing the forward cast in sooner and not allowing the backcast too much time to drop, or d) by putting *less* effort into the backcast if you are suffering from that over-powerful downwards flick of the rod tip as the butt is stopped at 12.30.

This fault is made much worse if there is a breeze blowing straight at your face (see Chapter 6).

LINE OR FLY HITS YOU

Firstly let us talk about the fly hitting you during the backcast, in other words it hits you in the face. A fly in the face is a recipe for disaster. If you are not wearing glasses or sunglasses you may well be blinded. It does not need a great big salmon fly to blind you – a size 16 dry fly, travelling fast, will rip an eyeball, leaving the jelly running down your cheek. It is a horrific sight which I have seen once, and hope I never see again. So wear glasses or sunglasses all the time you are fishing, even if it is raining.

The commonest cause of a line or fly hitting you, or the fly hitting the rod

This line has not landed straight. The wiggles are a symptom of a low backcast.

Raising the rod too far before putting in the flick of the backcast is a recipe for the fly coming back low, perhaps into your face. This position, if reached in dibbling a fly towards you, maybe in a boat, demands a roll cast for safety.

The 'Dog Nobbler Duck', often adopted by anglers using heavy flies on long flimsy leaders. There is an inbuilt urge to get the head out of the way of the fly as it comes forward too low. Shorten the leader, get the backcast up higher, and your neck will be safe at the end of a long day!

during the backcast, is lifting the rod too high before the flick is applied, or stopping the rod between the lift and the flick, allowing the line to sag before it is driven backwards. Lift the rod too high, say to 11 o'clock, and the line sags low in front of you, so it comes through low. The commonest symptom is for the fly to hit the rod somewhere in the top section. If it is a great big salmon fly, or a brass tube fly, it can sometimes have enough force to break the rod. More commonly it delaminates the carbon fibre layers during the impact, the delamination then slowly spreads in subsequent casts, and finally there is that loud crack and shower of black expensive bits around your ears. Do not hit tubular rods with a fast-moving fly – they do not like it, and it will cost you money in the end. (See D on page 29.)

The cure for the fly or line hitting you or the rod in the backcast is to put the power of the backcast in earlier. Done properly, the backcast should go up over the tip of the rod, and never come anywhere near you. Once you have started the backcast lift in motion, do not stop, whatever you do, as you have committed that fly on a path towards your face unless you keep the movement going upwards over the rod tip.

A fly in the back of the neck is an ecstatic experience. I once hit myself with a large brass salmon tube fly, and it felt as if I had been hit with a baseball bat. It fairly brings tears to your eyes, and anglers around our reservoirs know this. Which is why so many of them duck the head on every forward cast – a movement known as the 'Dog Nobbler Duck', and they end the day with a version of tennis neck. All because they throw a low backcast; which may come forward low. This is often combined with another fault, casting round the houses (see Line Twists, page 81).

If you throw a heavy fly low behind you, the odds are that it will go forwards low, and you are then standing in the way of it, so it hits you. Don't blame the weight of the fly – blame yourself for throwing it low behind in the first place. Throw it high behind and it will have even more momentum going downhill forwards, and will go much farther out towards where those trout are! Many anglers give themselves problems by tying a heavy fly, like a lead-head, on to a leader which is made too long and of too flimsy a nylon. If you watch a man trying to cast a lead-head on the end of 20 feet of 6-lb nylon you will see what I mean – he has no control over it, and it seems to have a mind of its own, malevolently directed at the back of his neck. A useful rule is that the heavier the fly then not only the *shorter* the leader, but also the *thicker* the leader. A lead-head fishes perfectly well on the end of 6 feet of 10-lb nylon, and is a dream to cast if you have never tried it. (And if your fly line is brown or green the fish won't mind at all!)

There is one instance when a high backcast produces a fly in the back, often either stuck in the hat, or between the shoulder blades (Sod's Law says that the only way you can remove this hook is to take your jacket off – and it is snowing!). If the forward cast is started off with a sharp jab, or a sharp wrist-flick, it can so collapse the spring of the rod that the line is flung *downwards* as it starts forwards. Standing beside an angler who suffers from this fault, it is fascinating to watch the fly flip just over his head time after time. Everything else about the cast can be perfect, but that little extra sharpness in the start of the forward cast dips the rod downwards

That little wiggle of loose line at the tip ring is a symptom of the rod being jerked to a stop in the backcast. Often combined – as in this case – with a dipping backcast. If the forward cast is started off with a flick instead of a gentle push, the fly will just flip over the head on the forward cast, or stick into the back of your hat, travelling fast!

before propelling the line forwards. I have seen some very good anglers suffering from this fault, and usually they were totally unaware of it.

There is also another instance. If the line is too heavy for the rod, or the rod is too soft for the weight of the line (which is another way of saying the same thing), the effort of flicking backwards or pushing forwards may well cause the rod to bend more without actually moving the tip backwards or forwards. This has the effect of dropping the line downwards instead of propelling it in a horizontal direction, and the resulting cast comes through low. This is a fault frequently suffered by owners of very old cane rods which have fatigued over the years, or of cheap glass rods which were perhaps sloppy to start with but which may also be suffering from fatigue of the resin. It is unusual to see carbon (graphite) rods suffering from this fault, but I have seen some long rods, say over 10½ feet, which did not have the inbuilt stiffness to handle the amount of line which the angler tried to aerialise. Do remember the AFTM number is a guide to the weight of *10 yards* of fly line outside the rod tip, and if you try to aerialise 15 yards, you are asking for this fault to occur and stick a hook in you. If you ever feel the rod bending under the cork handle you can be certain that you are over-loading the spring by trying to aerialise too much weight!

If somebody else's fly hits you, you should not have been there. Every angler has a danger area around him, and it is a self-imposed injury if you walk up to a man without warning him of your presence, or walk behind another angler without making sure he knows you are passing. Do not expect him to see you – he is concentrating on the fish out there, and has no thought that some idiot might wander into his backcast danger area.

In a boat, there is a golden rule. The man on the right-hand end of the boat casts over his right shoulder. The man at the left-hand end of the boat casts over his left shoulder. This is why left-handers are so much in de-mand as boat partners! If your partner is right-handed, make sure he casts to his left ear (see page 42). In a very large boat there may sometimes be another angler in the centre – he must be the man who does the best, highest backcast, vertically above his head, so that the only person in danger from his flies is himself. With only two anglers, or one angler and a ghillie, *the fly must never come over the boat* – even if circumstances dictate that you do all your fishing with a roll cast or Spey cast. You will know you are doing something wrong if the ghillie spends most of the day studying his toes, and turns up the next day wearing a motorcycle crash helmet and full face visor!

LINE LANDS WITH A SPLASH

This fault can have several versions. If the line is fully extended when it crashes down on to the surface, you aimed too low. Look at your right arm as you finish the forward cast – is it still bent? If it is, you chopped too much firewood for your old mum, and the habit of chopping downwards with the right hand is still with you. The arm must go out straight, with the right thumb tracking along an imaginary curtain rail. One end of this curtain rail is attached to your right ear, and the other end is somewhere above the horizon in front of you. Chopping downwards is a common

The forward cast has been delivered with an arm still bent. The thumb therefore tracked downwards instead of outwards, and so the line will go downwards. Here the symptom of the line landing near the rod first, and the fly landing last, is evident. The line is also landing hard enough to raise a splash, which makes trout extremely unhappy. 'Chopping firewood' is the shorthand for this fault!

Here the line has been shot while power was still on the rod, and it took all the guts out of the rod and all the tension out of the line – which is shimmying down onto the water, far short of its target.

habit among people who were taught to cast with a book under the upper arm, so that only the forearm and wrist could be moved, and the thumb was left no other path to follow except downwards. Cure this fault by simply raising your sights a bit, and aiming higher. Do not look at the water – look at the tops of the trees on the far side of the reservoir, or at any other imaginary aiming point which will cause the line to hover before it lands gently on the water.

Releasing line too soon on the shoot will sometimes cause the line to crash down on to the surface, but in this instance the line will not be fully extended anyway. By letting the line slip in the left hand while power is

Bowing to the fish results in everything going too low in front. The line is about to land near the tip and roll away along the surface, fly landing last.

still on the rod you take much of the power out of the cast, and the line will flop down on to the water. Do not release the shooting line until the tip of the rod has stopped.

Eagerness to get that line out there sometimes causes anglers to bow as they cast forwards. If you bow from the waist, everything will go too low in front, and the line will crash on to the surface while it is still travelling at speed. In addition to frightening the hell out of fish, this fault will give you a sore back and, if you have a tendency to arch your back every half an hour or so in search of relief from the pain, you are almost certainly bowing. I see no point in bowing to fish which are probably laughing at your attempts to fool them into taking your fly!

The same symptom will appear if the rod is drifted forwards while the backcast is rolling out behind. It is essential that the rod is kept motionless until the moment of starting the forward thrust. I know that some people advocate drifting the rod forward while the backcast is still going back, saying that this 'loads the rod ready for the forward cast'. If the rod is drifted forwards until it is at, say, 12 o'clock, and then the forward cast is started, you have left only the downwards component in the rod tip, and the cast will go downwards instead of outwards. Those people who advocate the drift have usually taken the rod very far back, thus allowing some forward drift while still leaving a horizontal component in the rod tip for the forward cast. Equally, by taking the rod so far back in the first place, they usually have too low a backcast. If you are casting for distance, by all means drift the rod tip while the line is rolling backwards, but drift it *backwards*, to give a longer application of power forwards. But to drift the rod tip forwards during the pause is a recipe for the line crashing on to the water before it has gone far enough.

The line can also be driven too low in front if the hand and arm are raised too high during the backcast. A forward cast started with the right hand higher than the head can only go downwards, because the thumb tracked downhill from that too-high position. If the thumb tracks downwards, the line will go downwards. If the thumb starts off in front of the ball of the shoulder, or somewhere beside the ear, it is physically possible for it to track in an upwards direction if required. Start the thumb off high above the head and it is physically impossible for it to go any other way but downwards by the time you run out of arm on the push. Do not confuse this high-arm backcast with a steeple cast (see Chapter 13) – I am here talking about the man who habitually casts a normal overhead cast by raising his right hand above his head. Even if by some miracle he manages to land the line gently, he will get tired very quickly, because the muscles which drive the extended arm forward are much smaller than the muscles which punch the fist forwards from shoulder height. To the man who suffers from this fault, I usually say – 'Keep your right elbow down during the backcast', and a cure is immediately apparent.

WIND KNOTS

Wind knots are caused by tailing loops. Tailing loops are caused by too much effort, which causes the tip of the rod to vibrate after the power of the cast has been stopped. This rod vibration is transferred to the line,

A very common casting fault, seen around every major stillwater. The hand is raised too high on the backcast, to a position from where it can only track downwards in the forward cast. This costs distance as the trajectory is too low. It also causes a very sore arm after 3 or 4 hours of this style.

The muscles which drive the arm forward from this position are very much smaller than the muscles which drive the arm forward from the ball of the shoulder. Would you start a punch from here?

These waves in the line are symptomatic of too much effort in the forward cast. The rod tip vibrates as it stops, sending a wave along the line. When the wave gets to the end, the leader flips back, forming a tailing loop. And tailing loops are a cause of wind knots.

Here the wrist was flicked in the backcast, and the tip of the rod is vibrating as it stops. This vibration sends waves along the line, forming wind knots in the backcast. The waves will not be evident until most of the line has turned over the rod tip, and cannot be seen by the angler unless he turns his head to look back.

causing waves to run along it. When the wave gets to the end, the fly flips back, dipping below the standing part of the line. There it may just hook on, often on the knot between line and leader, or the tail fly catches on a dropper fly, or the tail fly goes through the loop which it made when tailing and ties the simple thumb knot which anglers have come to call a wind knot. This is not caused by the wind, but by too much effort. The easy cure is to slacken the grip on the rod handle, as this takes some of the power out of the biceps and thus out of the cast. Wind knots can occur on both the backcast and the forward cast, but when there is a wind blowing in your face it is commonest for the knots to form in the forward cast, as that is where the excess effort is put in.

It is true to say that the stiffer the rod the less likely it is that you will get wind knots, because the vibrations of the tip are smaller, the waves along the line are smaller, and the tailing loop is smaller. There is thus less likelihood of the fly going through the loop. Remember, however, that a stiff rod becomes a softer rod when more weight is aerialised. This is common among anglers trying to cast farther – more line in the air, combined with more effort, both are calculated to increase the chance of wind knots.

The angler who cocks his wrist back a little is also more likely to give a little flick of the wrist on the forward thrust. This wrist-flick often contributes just the amount of extra effort needed to make the tip vibrate as it stops. So wrist-flick frequently causes wind knots. The initial cocking of the wrist in the backcast may well be flicked in, thus causing wind knots at the extremity of the backcast! See C on page 29.

LINE TWISTS

This problem is suffered by many reservoir anglers, who then blame the line maker for manufacturing a line which twists! I can assure you that line makers go to great lengths to see that their lines have no twists in them at any stage during the manufacturing process. Whatever price you pay for a fly line, it should come out of the box in beautifully neat coils and, providing you wind that line on to the reel properly (taking it off the coil in the same direction as mud would be flung from a wheel, turning the bulk coil as the line comes off), there will not be a single twist in it.

Go fishing with a 'round the houses' casting style, where the backcast comes back low and to the side, and the forward cast comes forward over the top of the rod, and the tip ring will collect a half-twist every backcast and every forward cast. These twists will migrate down through the rod rings, and will accumulate in the slack line between the butt ring and the reel. Then, when you want to shoot line, there will be a tangle of twisted line stuck in the butt ring and the line will not shoot. A quite famous angler has been heard to recommend that the reel should be taken off the rod every hour or so, and dangled until the line untwists itself! When I saw him casting with a sideways backcast and an overhead forward cast, I knew why he suffered the bugbear of line twists.

Please do not confuse these twists with the infuriating habit of one particular fly line, heavily advertised, which seems to go out straight, but

Line twists like this are not put there by the maker of the line, but by the angler who casts in a 'round the houses' style. This line will not shoot through the butt ring; it will tangle.

as soon as it lands slowly draws back into a series of spirals, the tips of which lie on the surface while the rest of each spiral sinks. After a few minutes there is no way a strike will reach the fly, as there is so much slack developed in the spirals. Most fly lines do not suffer from this infuriating habit and, if you have one which does, you should take it back and demand a return of your hard-earned money. Some fly lines, and the cheaper they are the more likely they are to suffer from this problem, tend after a while to lie on the surface with a little wiggle in them – there is nothing you can do about this except pull the line firmly through warm hands to straighten it – and some anglers feel that this is a benefit, as the straightening of a distant wiggle is often an indication of a take which might not have been noticed in a line lying dead straight.

I digress from line twists. These form in the shooting line inboard of the butt ring, and are caused by not casting back and forth in the same plane. A line which tracks back and forth over the tip of the rod does not suffer from twists, I assure you, and is going faster, and will give a higher backcast, which gives a faster and farther forward cast. All are very good reasons to school yourself to execute the backcast and the forward cast in the same plane.

LINE FAILS TO SHOOT

There are several possibilities here. The commonest cause of a failure to shoot is to let the shooting line go from the left hand too soon. If it is released even a split second before the rod tip stops, some of the power of the forward cast will be dissipated, and the line will not shoot as far as it should, even if it shoots at all. Please do not believe those instructors who tell you to shoot at 'the moment of maximum power'. Not only are they technically wrong, but the very phrase will encourage you to put too much effort into your casting. One symptom of letting go too soon is that the line will wrap around the blank inboard of the butt ring. Equally, if the line is shot too late, it will not go anywhere, as the forward momentum of the aerialised line will have died.

Failure to release the line altogether will cause extra friction, and the line will not shoot as far as it should. Forming an 'O' with the forefinger and thumb of the left hand, or merely slackening the grip and allowing the line to run over the palm of the left hand, are both habits which will cut down the shooting distance. Dump the fly line altogether out of the left hand, point the rod along the line of flight, and there will be only the friction through the butt ring to worry about – there is nothing you can do about this, provided that the butt ring is large enough. (If it is less than $\frac{1}{2}$ inch in diameter internally, you can change it for a bigger one.)

If you are *really* keen on maximising the distance you can shoot, it will pay you to study the rings on your rod, and think what happens to the fly line as it is shooting out through them. The line will be starting off perhaps from coils held in the left hand, or from a heap on the ground beside your left foot, or from coils laid in the water beside you. Suddenly accelerated

'Round the houses' style of casting, where the backcast is brought back to the side, and the forward cast is delivered over the top. Used by many anglers to overcome the tangles caused by tailing loops, and separate the planes of back and forward casts to avoid the line hitting itself. The resulting oval horizontal loop adds wind resistance. More power is thus needed to cast a given distance. Not only is there a high risk of broken hooks or flies lost in obstructions behind, but energy is being burned for nothing.

There is a style of casting, popularised by Lefty Kreh in the USA, which he calls a 'water haul'. The cast looks exactly like this, and is intended to kiss the fly and leader on the water at the extremity of the backcast. The resulting slight extra drag increases the spring of the rod on the forward delivery and adds distance. This style can only be used when there is a long clear stretch of water behind the angler.

upwards towards the butt ring, the line will be thrashing around in an uncontrolled fashion, until it is suddenly made to go through the butt ring. On the far side of the butt ring, this thrashing around repeats itself until the next ring is reached, when the line 'cones' again in order to get through the first of the intermediate rings. This is repeated all the way up the rod, with the 'coning' getting smaller all the time, but never being eliminated altogether. Between each ring, the coning causes the line to rub against the blank. With snake rings, the line is held very close to the blank in the first place, and the friction of the line rubbing against the blank is considerable. Full bridge rings, which hold the line farther away from the blank in the first place, yield less friction against the blank.

There is a way of reducing the coning of the line, and thus much of the friction of line rubbing against the blank. Fit two butt rings, 4 inches apart. The effect is to discipline the line immediately it has gone through those two butt rings, and it will go through the intermediates like an arrow. Many years ago I tried to sell reservoir rods fitted with these two butt rings, and on many occasions I had anglers telling me that they didn't 'look like fly rods' and they refused to buy them or even to enquire why the two rings were there. Commercial sense made me drop the idea and revert to selling fly rods which looked like the commonly accepted idea of a fly rod!

Back to the failure to shoot line. There remain two possibilities. One is that the line is tangled around a thistle, and the other is that you are standing on it! If you ever stand on your fly line, or the monofil running line behind a shooting head, stop and check. It is quite possible that you have cut it, and your next cast will go out of sight over the horizon. When you realise that all that money is flying away from you the language will be awful. It pays to check the line where your big foot trod on it.

PAIN

You may be surprised to see pain put down here as a casting fault. One of my very good friends told me recently that he had just fished hard for two consecutive days and, on the following morning, he had had to shave with two hands, as he could not raise his right hand on its own up to his chin! Don is a superb fly tier, a totally dedicated angler, but he casts with his right hand waving up above his head. For those two days he was locked into using a shooting head and casting as far as he could, with painful results. If he could only school himself to cast at shoulder height, not only would he cast farther, but it would be with less muscular effort.

Pain in the forearm is a symptom of gripping the rod too tightly.
Pain across the shoulders is a symptom of gripping too tightly with both hands.
Pain in the wrist is a symptom of flexing the wrist too much. A wrist which hardly moves while casting will not hurt.
Pain across the forehead is a symptom of your shirt collar being too tight, or an indication that you should wear sunglasses before staring at the ripple all day!

11
THE SLACK LINE CAST

Seldom used on reservoirs, but desirable sometimes on rivers, the slack line cast deliberately lands slack line in wiggles in front of the angler. Imagine standing on a riverbank, looking over a fast current at a fish rising under the far bank. If you cast a nice straight line, your fly will be whipped away from the target area by the drag of the current in the middle of the river, probably before the fish has a chance to take it. How do you cast to

The slack line cast is designed to land line in a wiggle in front of you. In this photograph, the leader has not yet landed.

the target area, but with some slack line in the middle of the river for the current to drag at, leaving the fly stationary over that fish for as long as possible? The answer is the slack line cast.

Do a normal overhead cast and, immediately the rod stops after the forward push, waggle the rod tip from side to side, with the rod tip going to a position each side of the line of delivery by about 2 feet. It isn't a little shiver of the rod tip, it is a positive waggle, 2 feet either side. The effect is to send a series of waves along the fly line, which land as slack 'sine-waves' on the water.

If you waggle early, the waves will have more time to travel away from you along the line, and the farther away from you will the slack land. Waggle late, and the slack will be nearer to the rod tip. Position the slack so that it is over the current, and your fly will stay in the target area without drag for as long as possible.

The slack line cast is one of those casts which, once seen or explained is so easy you wonder why you didn't think of it yourself!

12
THE REACH CAST

More controlled than the slack line cast, the *reach* cast is designed to lay a neat belly of fly line to the side of the line from you to the target. Anybody can do it after being shown once.

Do a normal overhead cast and, as the forward push stops, reach arm, hand and rod out to the side and back again. Time it so that the rod comes back to the target line at the same moment as the fly line actually lands.

The reach cast lands line in a loose belly, whichever side of the direction of the target you choose. If you have a problem with this cast, you are probably trying to hurry. Give yourself more time by aiming slightly higher, to allow more time for the reach to the side and back before the line lands.

The result is a big belly of fly line lying on the water, but the fly will have landed in line with the original direction of delivery, although a bit nearer than it would have been without the slack in the belly.

The reach cast can be done to left or to right. It gives the ideal starting point for mending line for a drag-free drift of the fly.

Any difficulty I have had with beginners in learning this cast has been caused by the innate desire to hurry. The movements should be almost ponderous, as there is plenty of time between the end of the push and the line actually landing for that gentle reach out and back with the rod tip.

13
THE STEEPLE CAST

People come to me to be taught the steeple cast, and seem dismayed when I tell them that I cannot remember the last occasion I used it in actual fishing conditions. I think it was on a little chalk stream many years ago, when I had to stand in shoulder-high rushes in order to fish. There was a high bank behind, with a barbed wire fence running along the top. For concealment, I had to stand well back in the rushes, and I was at least half a rod-length back from the water. There was only one possible place for a backcast, and that was straight up. My host Charles, a lovely man, walked half a mile downstream, crossed by a plank bridge, and walked half a mile back, then knelt down and fished the same pool from the clear bank opposite! His mixture of apology at not realising that he was casting over my line together with incredulity that I could cast from so impossible a spot was comical to hear, and I pulled his leg about it for years afterwards.

The steeple cast is not the easiest of casts to get right. The backcast must go high in the air, almost straight up from the rod tip. Because the forward cast starts so high, there is a dreadful tendency for the line to crash down on to the surface in front of you.

Start by lifting the right elbow out sideways, so that the upper arm is parallel to the ground. Now drop the rod tip to the water surface, and pull out any slack with the left hand. Rotate the whole of the right hand so that the thumb is below the rod and the back of the hand is facing you. Do a very short lift, blended into a strong flick upwards, all carried out by rotating only the upper arm. Stop the rod absolutely vertically. All these slightly contorted movements will fling the line almost vertically upwards above the rod tip and, done powerfully enough, the line will extend fully up there.

Then comes the problem of how to prevent the line rushing downhill into the water. Remember that the line will go where the right thumb goes, and you want it to go outwards, not downwards. The solution is to rotate the right hand so that the thumb is behind the rod for the forward cast, drop the elbow right down to the waist, with the right thumb in front of the ball of the shoulder, and drive the forward cast in a strongly upwards direction. This repositioning of the right arm is all done while the upcast is flowing upwards – do not give the line time to drop or you will be in all sorts of trouble.

The steeple cast is a short line cast. Ten yards of line, plus whatever

The steeple cast. Start with the rod tip touching the water. Lift the elbow out sideways, and turn the wrist so that the thumb is under the grip. This will rotate the butt of the rod so that the reel is uppermost. Shooting line is almost impossible during a steeple cast.

Flick the backcast upwards by rotating the upper arm from the ball of the shoulder. I find it difficult to do this without the wrist turning slightly. Ideally, at the position photographed, the thumb should still be on the forwards side of the grip. The backcast is now sailing up into the air, as vertically above the rod as possible.

While the backcast is flowing upwards, drop the elbow as low as possible, turn the wrist so that the thumb is behind the grip, and get ready, all in one movement, to aim *high* in front.

This forward thrust could, with advantage, have been aimed higher, say level with the peak of the cap, or the top of the head.

leader you fancy, is as much as even a very good caster will cope with in a true steeple cast. Start practising with 7 yards of line outside the rod tip.

While it is worth knowing how to do the steeple cast and putting it in the bank for a rainy day, there are very few occasions when a roll cast would not be more efficient and easier to execute. The steeple cast 'impresses the natives'. The roll cast catches more fish for me.

14
THE SIDE CAST

Useful under trees and overhanging branches, under bridges, or even for casting sideways into the teeth of an along-shore gale, the side cast is only an overhead cast laid on its side. The same clock face is used, but with 12 o'clock at right angles (either to the right or the left) to the line to the target, instead of vertically.

Start in the same position as for an overhead cast, with the line out in front of you, rod tip low, and no slack under the rod tip. Roll the right hand and forearm to the right, so that, while the rod is still pointing at the target, the back of the hand is facing downwards. (You should now be looking at your fingernails.) The result of rolling the hand to the right is that the rod will now bend in the plane it is meant to, with the rings on the inside or outside of the curve of the blank when it is bent. Now lock the right elbow into the waist, and lock the wrist too.

Turn the upper body to the right, slowly at first to give the equivalent of the lift to 10 o'clock, then accelerating for the flick backwards. Stop the shoulders at the moment the tip of the rod reaches an imaginary 12.30 position, and the backcast is completed. The rod tip should track backwards in a slightly rising plane so that, as the backcast is complete, the tip of the rod is about the same height from the ground as your shoulders. By doing the backcast by turning from the waist, and not just with the arm, you lock up when the rod has reached the correct stopping point and it is almost impossible to bring the rod too far back. If the rod goes too far back in the backcast, the fly will drop on the way *forward* and may touch the ground.

Allow slightly less time for the backcast to unroll than you would in an overhead cast. No great harm will result if the fly is brought around the corner sharply, because, with only a short line out, no great force is being applied anyway, and the fly is unlikely to crack off.

The forward cast is a gentle turning from the waist to bring the rod back to pointing at the target. The elbow is still locked against the waist.

Once half a dozen casts have been made, and you have grasped firmly in your mind where 12.30 is, and seen the results of not stopping the rod there at the extremity of the backcast, a much more relaxed style can be adopted, using the whole arm and keeping the shoulders still. For this relaxed style, it pays to have the left foot forward and the left shoulder pointing at the target. It is then possible to watch the whole of the cast

The side cast – at the extremity of its backcast. Notice how the hand is turned on its side, fingernails upwards, resulting in the rod also being on its side. If it should be necessary to watch the backcast rolling out, make sure the left foot and left shoulder are leading.

The side cast on the left. Back of the hand on top, right foot leading.

going back and forth, and to keep it under control. As a further advance, you can kneel down and try a few casts from that position – if you fish in small streams it is surprising how often you will find this useful. It is essential, though, that all side casts are done with the hand on its side, both backcast and forward cast.

An aid to accuracy is the wrist-turn. As the rod reaches a direct line to the target at the end of the forward thrust, turn the hand sharply to bring the thumb on top. The effect of this is to make the last part of the uncocking movement of the spring of the rod take place downwards instead of forwards. This throws the line downwards, takes the horizontal error out of the rod tip and line, and the line will land like an arrow pointing at the target. Not to be used with a dry fly without some practice, as it tends to make the fly land hard unless you aimed high in the first place, but very useful for accurate placement of a wet fly or nymph.

For a side cast to the left, called by some the backhanded side cast, start by turning the right hand on to its other side, with the back of the hand on top. Lay the imaginary clock face over on to your left side. Keeping the back of the hand on top during the backcast and the forward cast, do a mirror of what you did on the right but this time on your left. Want to watch the line? Then lead with the right shoulder.

For casting farther with a side cast, try the effect of a double-haul and shooting line. With a little practice you will be amazed at how far you can cast, even though the line is tracking back and forth below shoulder height. With a weight-forward line you should be able to aerialise 10 yards and shoot 6 yards. With a 9-foot rod and a 9-foot leader you will now be casting 22 yards from your toes to the fly.

Just about the only thing which can go wrong with a side cast is that the fly touches the ground or water. If it touches at the extremity of the back-cast, you simply threw it too low – raise the plane of the backcast slightly. If the fly touches on the way forwards, you took the rod back too far in the backcast – remember where 12.30 is and stop the backcast there.

One last point. Having got yourself under that tree and decided that the only cast possible is a side cast, don't forget in the heat of the moment and strike upwards, or you will do your rod a mischief against the branches!

Side cast on the left completed. Notice that the back of the hand is still on top. If the wrist is rolled upright *while the rod is coming forwards*, the cast will inevitably land too low. If, on the other hand, the wrist is rolled upright at the moment the rod completes the forward cast (and not before), the cast will be more accurate.

15
THE CURVE CAST

A variation of the side cast, the curve cast is intended to land the line in a deliberate curve, so as to present the fly to a fish upstream of you without laying the leader over its back in the process.

Imagine you are stalking a rising fish in a crystal-clear stream. You approach from behind the fish, from downstream. If you lay a nice straight cast, putting the fly a foot upstream of its nose, the leader will land right up its back and in the window of vision directly above its eyes. Not a good idea!

A better idea is to cast so that the fly lands a foot upstream of its nose, but the leader comes in from the side, or even from a little upstream. To do this a curve cast is needed, and it does require a good deal of practice to master.

Basically a curve cast is a side cast, overpowered a bit on the forward delivery. This will cause the leader to curve around before it lands. If a right-hand side cast is done, the leader will curve to the left. To curve the leader to the right, do a left-hand side cast.

I have found that the easiest way to teach the curve cast is just to tell the student to aim a side cast a fraction higher and to put a little more effort into the delivery. After a couple of shots at it, they usually get it right. On the few occasions when this particular analogy will not work, I try suggesting a little backwards tug of the tip ring, just as the side cast is about to turn the leader over. If that doesn't work, I suggest a little pull with the left hand on the line, again just as the cast is about to turn the leader over. One of these three methods will produce a curve in the final delivery.

I would strongly suggest that this cast be practised before you try it on the biggest fish of the season, as it seldom goes correctly the first time you try it. If you are a little rusty, and are looking at that huge fish, try a couple of casts a few feet off-target to the side before you ring the dinner bell for Charlie.

16
THE ROLL CAST

This cast, which most anglers cannot do properly, is still one of the most useful of all the fishing casts.

Standing with your back against a cliff, bridge, high bank or dam wall, this cast will put the fly out in front of you with no danger of broken hooks. Fishing a deeply sunk line, it is the cast which will put the line up into the air in front of you, ready for an overhead cast without risking a broken rod or a fly in the face. These are all advantages held by the roll cast, yet so few anglers know how to do it well.

Perhaps because of all the nonsense they have read about this cast, they never get it right. Some examples:

'Lift the rod vertically in front of your face and thrash the tip downwards to roll the line out onto the surface in front of you.'
'Raise the hand above your head and whip the tip of the rod smartly down onto the water – you will see the whole line roll along the surface until it is all extended.'
'Roll casting can only be done on water, and cannot be practised on grass.'
'All the line must be in front of the angler at the moment of downward delivery.'

All of these statements carry a basic misconception which will actively prevent a student ever being able to do a nice roll cast. It baffles me why the average writer or angler should think that a roll cast *has* to roll along the surface, creating disturbance which frightens fish. Why should a roll cast not roll the line out *above* the surface, where it can hover and land gently, just as we try to do with every other cast?

Perhaps we had better start by going back to those two first principles which we discussed:

1) Without a good backcast you cannot get a good forward cast.
2) The line will go where the thumb goes.

These principles apply to the roll cast as well as to all the others, so why all the insistence upon the hand thrashing *downwards* on the *forward* roll cast? No wonder many anglers, faced with all this contradictory instruction, find the roll cast a frustrating experience. Yet it is so easy.

The roll cast is split into two parts, the backcast and the forward cast. Let us get the backcast right first.

Imagine you are standing on the bank, your line is extended out in front of you on the surface. You are quite relaxed, and it does not matter where your feet are, but your shoulders are facing your target. If you want to cast more line than is outside the rod tip, strip off the reel and waggle the rod tip to slide line out through the rings, so that all the line you want to cast is now outside the tip ring. This is quite important, as it is very difficult to shoot line in a roll cast – and much easier to get it outside the tip ring in the first place. (This waggle is how you get the line out to start with if you are in a tight corner with a cliff behind you.)

Now draw the rod slowly back, leaning it to the right as you do so. Keep the right hand coming back until you are at full arm-stretch behind and to your right. Do this slowly, so that the line is drawn slowly back, sliding along the surface towards you, and the sag of line is laid on the bank beside you, *half a rod-length away from your feet*. It is essential for your safety that the line is not lying close to your feet as, on delivery of the forward cast, the fly starts off by coming towards you. Lay the line close beside you and the fly may well stick in you as you execute the forward cast – usually under the chin, which is a delightful experience. You are now standing with your shoulders turned to your right, right arm outstretched behind you, and as much line as possible laid behind your feet. The fly is still in the water in front of you, and it will now slide to a stop. You have all the time in the world for this gentle drawing back to full arm-stretch.

Now turn to face your target again, and drop the right elbow so that your right hand is right in front of the ball of the right shoulder. Now look at the rod, and set it up pointing to 2 o'clock. Your wrist will be cocked a little, you notice. The rod must also be lying slightly out to the right, so that the tip ring is vertically over the line to which it is going to give momentum in the forward cast. This setting up is the most important part of the roll cast – get it wrong, and the cast cannot go in the direction you require.

If the rod is set up too far back, pointing say to 3 o'clock, whatever you do with your thumb on the forward cast, that line will go too high, as the rod tip has to start off by going upwards.

If the rod is set up too far forward, say at 12 o'clock, whatever you do with your thumb on the forward cast, the line will go too low, landing near you first and running away along the surface, finishing with a splash as the fly and leader land – you left only the downwards component of the rod tip when you set the rod up.

Set the rod up at 2 o'clock and, by driving your thumb out straight, aimed slightly above the horizontal, to full arm-stretch, you will drive the tip ring, and thus the line, *outwards* in front of you. The line will extend fully, the leader will straighten, and then all will land together, and gently, upon the water.

Let us summarise. The backcast involves drawing the line back slowly, turning from the waist, to point the rod as far behind you as you can reach, and laying the line say 4 or 5 feet to your right. Then turn to face your target, drop the elbow, and set the rod up at 2 o'clock. That completes the backcast, and you can stay in that position as long as you like – there is no need to hurry.

There is a thing in fishing called Sid's Law. This says that you will get a rise just at the moment you are at full arm-stretch backwards, and have no

The roll cast as often described. 'Lift the rod upright and thrash the tip forwards and downwards.' WRONG.

If the forward thrust is downwards, the line will land hard and not go very far. Line bashing onto the water surface will scare fish over long distances.

more arm to strike with. Easy – strike by driving the tip of the rod *forwards*. This will bring the fly back towards you, and stick the hook in. Then lift the rod up, take the slack out, and start playing the fish. It does require immense willpower to strike towards the fish, so rehearse it in your mind from time to time so that it becomes an automatic reaction when that rise eventually happens.

Having set the rod up, with the right thumb *no higher* than your ear, preferably in front of the ball of the right shoulder, you are ready for the forward cast. This is a straight punch with the right thumbnail leading, aimed at a point slightly higher than horizontal, out to full arm-stretch. If you end up with a bent elbow, you chopped firewood, and the cast will go too low. Stick your thumb in his eye, and his eyeball is on top of the trees on the far side of the reservoir!

If the line goes out so far, and then the rest shimmies down in a heap, you aimed too high. Either you aimed your thumb at too high a point, or you set the rod up too far back.

If the line near the rod lands first, and the rest runs away along the surface, with the fly landing hard, you aimed too low. Either you aimed your thumb at too low a point, or you set the rod up too vertically.

So every time you set the rod up, look at it. Make sure you standardise on that 2 o'clock position, and then any error of elevation can be corrected by raising or lowering your aiming point in front. If the rod didn't start from a standard position, you will not know where you are.

Direction of delivery is important. With the belly of the backcast laid to your right, you must not aim to the right of the line on the water, or you will cross over and tangle on the delivery. You must aim to the left, or directly above, the line on the water.

Suppose, however, you want to deliver the fly to your right. You must form the belly of the backcast on your left. Easy. Turn from the waist to the left. Reach your right thumb as far to the left and behind you as you can, laying that line 4 or 5 feet away from your feet. Turn back to face your target, leaving the rod leaning to the left. Set yourself up with the right thumb right in front of your eyes, to act as an imaginary backsight. Look at the rod and ensure it is leaning back at 2 o'clock. Now, with the back of the right hand staying on top, stick your thumb in his eye across the reservoir. If you rotate the hand as you drive the thumb forward, the cast will go too low – the back of the hand *must* stay on top until the forward cast is completed. The same principle applied to the overhead cast done on your left-hand side, remember?

Whichever side you laid the backcast, as soon as the forward thrust of the thumb is completed, drift down with the rod and relax your right elbow. Your line will now all be lying out on the water in front of you, straight, having landed gently.

If the line goes out and hovers 1 foot above the water, then lands like thistledown, you did the roll cast correctly. Anything else is just sloshing and bashing without understanding the principles behind the cast.

Remember that the rod gives forward momentum only to the loose line in that belly, or capital D, lying behind the rod. There has to be enough momentum given to that loose line to pick up and carry out all the rest of

The roll cast, also wrong. Bring the rod too far back like this, and the tip can only go upwards in the forward cast. The line will go too high, and shimmy back onto the water in a heap. Notice also how the line is too close to the legs, giving the unpleasant possibility of a fly stuck firmly into your person.

The roll cast, the correct way. Start by reaching slowly back to full arm-stretch to the right rear. This puts as much line as possible behind the rod when it is set up for the forward cast. Notice how all the rest of the line stays lying out in front of the angler . . .

99

the line, the leader and the fly. It follows that the greater the proportion of line there is behind the rod, the better the roll cast will go. The most efficient cast is where *all* the line is behind the rod – as in an overhead cast. The least efficient cast is where there is *no* line behind the rod – which is exactly what is suggested by those misguided souls who suggest that you lift the rod to the vertical and then thrash the line downwards!

Roll casting does require a fair amount of effort. If half the line is behind the rod, you have to apply twice the power that you would use in an overhead cast. If only a quarter of the line is behind the rod, you have to apply *four times* the power. For this reason, if there is room behind you, you can nudge a little more line into that belly behind if you wish. Or, if you have slack in your hand, you can shoot a little of it while you are forming the belly behind, and it will slide out through the rings and form a larger capital D – then your forward delivery will go even better.

There is one other method of making that forward cast go even better, and that is to give a single-haul on the forward cast. When you are setting yourself up at 2 o'clock, have both hands together in front of the ball of the shoulder, with no slack between your left hand and the butt ring. As the right hand starts the forward thrust, the left hand pulls sharply downwards and then lets go to shoot the small amount of line pulled. This is an effective way to roll cast into a wind, as it speeds up the delivery and punches the line out. If there is anything more than a gentle breeze in your face, you also aim your thumb at a slightly lower eyeball out there, or set the rod up at 1 o'clock instead of 2 o'clock.

The roll cast can also be laid on its side, and becomes a sideways roll cast – useful under trees – and this can be done on either side of the body.

One last point. If you have any loose line inside the butt ring at the moment of starting the forward cast, it will rap your knuckles. Not all that important on a nice warm summer's day, but if you are roll casting with a salmon rod in February (euphemistically called spring fishing!), when there is a grue of ice coming down the river and your hands are all one big hurt, this slapping of the line against the back of the fingers will bring tears to your eyes.

The roll cast is a most useful cast. When I am wet fly fishing in a river, I have spent whole days roll casting, with never an overhead cast at all. It saves a lot of worry about trees reaching out for the flies, and it allows me to fish in places which other anglers walk past, telling themselves that there is no room for casting. The fish in those places have seen fewer flies, and are thus easier to catch.

When dry fly fishing, I have sometimes been frustrated beyond belief by the Catch 22 situation. Roll casting is the only way to reach that fish. Roll casting does not dry the fly sufficiently for reliable flotation, even when single-hauled on the delivery. The answer is to get it right first time and catch the fish with the first cast, and I wish I could do it!

Now to the sunk line. I sigh when I hear somebody being advised to 'roll the line to the surface, and then pick it off in an overhead cast before it has time to sink'. Why all the surface disturbance? Why not roll the line out in front of you, but up in the air, and pick it back into an overhead backcast before it has time to touch the water?

. . . Now drop the elbow – this is most important. Set the thumb beside the right ear, and check that the rod is pointing to between 1 and 2 o'clock. Look at a point above the horizon, and drive the right thumb at it to full arm-stretch. This photo shows the backcast completed, with a nice large capital D of line behind the rod.

Correctly done, the roll cast will roll the line out *above* the surface, so that it settles like thistledown. Just like any other cast, your line should all land at the same time along its length.

The roll cast on the left-hand side of the body, designed to throw the forward cast to the right of the line on the water. Start by reaching as far to the left rear as possible, turning from the waist to do so . . .

. . . Now drop the right elbow, use the right thumb as a backsight, check the rod is set up at around 2 o'clock and leaning to the left, and drive the thumb outwards and slightly upwards.
It will be noticed that, in the photograph, the back of the hand is on top. (If you touch your thumbnail to your nose you will see that the back of the hand is on top.)

Keeping the back of the hand on top all the way, drive the thumbnail outwards to full arm-stretch. The impetus given to the loose belly of line (the capital D) will pick up all the rest and roll it out above the water, where it will hover and settle gently. The spray from the line picking off the water can be clearly seen.

The hands are held quite close together to give the single haul on the delivery of a roll cast. Here the capital D has been formed, and the forward cast has just been started. The foreshortening effect of the lens is apparent here – there are over 10 yards of line lying on the water (and it looked straight from where the author was standing!).

All you have to do is to aim high on the forward delivery – and I mean high – up at 45° high, and immediately you have delivered you bring the rod back smartly to 12.30. This will drive a nice high backcast behind you ready for an effortless forward cast and shoot. What, no false cast, I hear you say? No, no false casting, or, if you really have pulled in a lot of line on the retrieve, maybe *one* false cast, no more. When you first try this roll cast to get a sunk line in the air, remember that the commonest error is to cock the wrist on the overhead backcast, throwing the line low behind. It takes a certain amount of muscle discipline not to bring the rod back past 12.30.

By following this suggested method of roll casting, you will be able to cast a line which lands like thistledown on the water. Or on grass. If you do it in the way I have described, you will be able to roll cast on grass, and win as many beers as I have from those who say you cannot do it except on water. They belong to the 'lift to 12 and thrash down' brigade, and that dictum makes it impossible on grass and horrible on water!

17
CHANGING DIRECTION

It is said that every problem is a solution in disguise. To the average angler standing on the bank, a fish rising is an opportunity, but if his fly is not already somewhere in the vicinity of that feeding fish, the problem is often more apparent than the solution. How to pick the fly off the water and deliver it in a totally different direction to cover that fish, before the damn thing has time to swim away?

Most anglers I have seen burn a lot of energy, and frighten the fish, in the attempt to cover a rising fish. The usual method is to pick the fly line off the water into a backcast, in line with where the fly came from, then turn slightly and do a false cast, then turn some more and do another false cast, then turn some more and do yet another false cast. When eventually the line is flickering over the fish's last known location, there is one more false cast for luck, and the fly is finally put down where the rise was seen, or just upwind of it. (Fish always travel upwind when feeding, don't they?) By which time the fish is long gone, and all that exercise was in vain. The easy solution seems so well disguised that very few anglers have ever heard of it.

Imagine you are standing facing the water and your line is out on the surface, half-right from where you are looking. A fish rises to your half-left. This involves a 90° change of angle between where the line is and where you want it to go. Turn from the waist and point the rod at the rise, with the tip of the rod only a couple of inches from the surface or, better still, touching the water. Do one backcast and one forward cast in the direction of the rise, and the fly will go there!

Notice I said *one backcast and one forward cast*. No false casting whatever, unless you want to frighten the fish with a line flickering back and forth in the air over its head. It is as simple as – point the rod, one backcast and deliver the fly to the rise. Total time elapsed about 1½ seconds. There is no time for the target fish to swim away. There is only time for the fish to think, 'That's a tasty mouthful. Oh, another one!' and, without further ado, it will take your fly. You will put a lot of fish in the bag by using this technique.

On the other hand, a fish swimming along and seeing your fly sitting there is likely to think, 'Ah, a black gnat. Funny, this one has a silver rib, and all the ones I have eaten this morning had gold ribs. Hell, it's got nylon tied to it. No, thank you!' and away it swims, leaving your fly undisturbed. I can assure you that probably hundreds of fish a day do this, and you never know, unless you fish in crystal-clear water and can see everything going on before your very eyes.

The way to catch nothing at all is to false cast on a sunny day. The wet fly line, whatever its colour, will flash in the sunlight, and every fish underneath it will take off for pastures new. I like to tell the story of the B52 bomber coming across the Atlantic. Every member of the crew had an ejector seat, and half-way across, there was a bang and out went the flight engineer. A stunned silence for a moment, and there was another bang and the rear gunner ejected. The rescue search found only the rear gunner, who was asked during his de-briefing why he had ejected, as there was nothing wrong with the aeroplane. 'Well', he said. 'I heard Charlie go, and I guessed he knew something I didn't.' A fish, seeing another fish fleeing from an unknown threat, is most likely to go with it. The alternative is to stay around and get eaten by whatever frightened Charlie.

False casting, therefore, may not frighten your target fish, but if it frightens another, which flees and takes your target fish with it, the effect is the same – you will not catch anything. False casting should be avoided at all times unless absolutely necessary.

Should you aim to the upwind side of the rise? In my opinion you should not. It is my belief that only certain things make fish feed only in an upwind direction, and a wind lane is one example of what *might* make fish feed with their noses permanently into wind. A stream of insects being blown off a point of land might be another. But most of the trout I have studied wander around looking for food, rather aimlessly it seems. They remind me of a small boy on a beach looking for a lost coin, going a yard here, a yard there, and every now and then looking up to see where he is, and going back to his chosen starting point.

Looking at a rising fish, one often says – 'There's a fish, and it's going left'. What you actually saw was a fish which happened to be facing left as it broke surface and took a mouthful. You jump to the conclusion that it will stay heading in that same direction while you cast to it. Very often it will follow a descending spiral from the surface and be heading in quite another direction by the time it is back to its hunting depth. Many fish will break surface heading into wind because that is the best way to ensure that the insect is not going to get away. The insects are being blown downwind, and the best interception course is one which faces the way the food is coming from. The fish may well not have been travelling upwind when it first saw the insect, but rose in a climbing spiral to take the upwind mouthful.

I have found that the best way to maximise the chances of the fish thinking 'Oh, another one' is to put the fly bang into the centre of the rise rings. By aiming off, you actually increase the chances of guessing wrongly and, if you are wrong, you double the distance between your fly and the fish. By putting the fly in the centre of the rings of the rise, you increase the chances of the fish thinking, 'Oh, there must have been two of them', and taking yours! But to succeed in this, your fly must land as soon as ever

To change direction, ignore
where the line actually is.
Point the rod to the new
target, and touch the tip on the
water. Ensure there is no slack
under the rod tip.

Do one backcast, stopping the
rod at 12.30. The photograph is
slightly deceptive – be assured
that the backcast is as high as
the tip of the rod!

Do one forward cast, aimed forward at shoulder height . . .

. . . And the line goes straight to the new target! Total time elapsed about 1½ seconds, and no energy wasted in false casting.

possible after the fish took the first mouthful. Even with a short line out, every false cast will cost you over a second. A trout cruising looking for food can cover over 3 feet a second.

Back to the cast which will put your fly over that fish in less than 2 seconds, every time. Firstly, judge by eye how much line you need. If you have too much line out of the tip ring, pull some in over the forefinger of the right hand. As soon as you have the correct amount, point the rod at the rise. It does not matter where the rise took place, if it is within 90° of your fly, point the rod at the rise, and touch the tip ring on the water. Now do one backcast, making sure you stop the rod at 12.30. If a very large change of direction is needed, put the power of the flick in a little earlier, say at 9.30 instead of at 10 o'clock. You will thus get a nice high backcast while the rod sorts out the change of direction being taken by the line. Pause for a fraction of a second longer than during a straight backwards and forwards cast, because the line will be going around in a circular course behind you instead of straight back and forth, and that takes a little longer. If you have a lot of line out, you should grip the handle a fraction tighter than normal, as the rod will be trying to twist in your hands a little.

If you have too little line outside the tip ring when you see the rise, pull some line off the reel over the little finger of your right hand, and shoot it on the delivery. Still no false casting, just one shoot.

This idea of pointing the rod first in order to do a change of direction, however large a change, is so simple, so quick, and the results so effective, that you will wonder why you never thought of it before. I have seen a review of a rod saying what a marvellous rod it must be to be able to change direction like this – nothing at all to do with the rod (although the rod being reviewed was indeed a superb rod) but everything to do with following the two golden rules I mentioned right at the very beginning of this book – a good backcast, and the line going where the tip of the rod goes.

Many anglers trying to change direction will pick up from the direction in which the line is lying, turn and deliver in the direction they want the line to go, and see the fly crash on to the water hard in front of them every time. The error they commit is simple. They put a nice straight backcast up behind them to start with, but then they turn and deliver in a different direction. By doing this, much of the power of the forward cast is used up in re-aligning the track of the rod tip. The rod is thus twisted as it delivers the forward push, and a rod which has been twisted as well as bent has much less power than a rod just bent. It is impossible to change the direction of the line in the air by more than a few degrees at a time, known by the man who false casts so much.

So much for the overhead change of direction. There is another way which takes a fraction longer, but which is useful if there are obstructions behind. The double-Spey cast is covered in Chapter 19 but applies also to the single-handed rod. This cast will also change the direction of the line by up to 90°, and will do so without frightening fish. This is most useful for the wet fly angler on a stream or river, who has the constant job of taking the fly from below him in the current, called 'on the dangle' and putting it back across the river. With no obstructions behind, the overhead cast 'point the rod and do one cast' will work every time, but with bushes, trees, or a high bank behind, the double-Spey is the cast to use.

18

THE DOUBLE-HANDED
ROD

Every cast I have described so far, except for double-hauling, can be done with a double-handed rod. The principles are all exactly the same, as the mechanics do not change just because the length of the spring is increased. A salmon rod is only a longer spring, which, because of its greater weight, is easier to wield with two hands instead of with only one.

The grip on a salmon rod with the right hand is almost exactly the same as on a trout rod. The line is trapped under the little finger, and under the forefinger, in exactly the same way, and for the same reasons. The right thumb should be as high up the handle as is comfortable, and most cork grips have a swelling up near the top, designed as a rest for the ball of the right thumb. Bear in mind that the farther apart the hands are, the more leverage you can exert, and the easier the application of power becomes. If you hold the rod with both hands close together, one on either side of the reel, you make hard work of casting.

If your hands on a 15-foot salmon rod are 1 foot apart, the leverage you exert is 1 to 14. If the hands are 2 feet apart, the leverage becomes 2 to 13, or 1 to 6½, and you are increasing to a considerable degree the mechanical disadvantage. You will get a lot less tired if your hands are as far apart as you can manage without stress. Just occasionally one comes across a salmon rod which has apparently been made for a gorilla, but most well-thought-out rods these days have a handle whose total length, from the button to the top of the corks, is around 26 inches. This length has been evolved over the years as being about right for the man, or woman, of average build.

The left-hand grip is something about which there seems to be some controversy. I have seen it suggested that the butt button should be poised on the fingertips of the left hand. I find it impossible to have much control of the rod with this flimsy grip, and advise against it. Another suggestion is that the button should be cupped in the palm of the left hand. This, I find, gives me a blister in a place where the skin is thin, tender, and unused to pressure or friction, right in the centre of the palm. There is, in my view, only one way to hold the rod with the left hand, and that is to get a grip of it. While as a basic rule the left hand merely takes the weight of the rod, leaving the right hand to do the work, there are occasions when you want to pull with the left hand as the right hand drives the rod outwards, and this is impossible with any other form of grip.

An incorrect grip on a double-handed rod. The fingertips of the left hand do not give enough grip or control.

Holding the rod in the palm of the left hand will cause blisters.

Having the hands too close together increases the amount of effort required to cast by a dramatic degree. To hold any part of the line in the left hand is asking for a tangle around the reel or reel handle on every shoot.

The correct grip, holding the rod gently but firmly. Note how the line trapped by the little finger, tight to the reel, stays under control. To shoot line on the forward cast, simply point the forefinger.

One also sees it suggested that the loose line (the line to be shot) is held in both hands, and not trapped only under a finger of the uppermost hand. By holding the line near the rod with the left hand, you are asking for the line to be trapped around the reel as soon as you shoot it. At best it will catch around the reel handle. At worst it will catch around the back of the spool. Both are annoying, and can cost you a fish – it is no time to be worrying about untangling line from around the reel when you have 20 lb of angry muscle heading seawards! Keep things simple and organised and tangles are less likely. But still develop the habit of glancing at the line between the reel and the butt ring after every single cast!

We will now run through the casting sequence for a standard overhead cast with a salmon fly rod. Stand relaxed, shoulders facing your target square-on. It does not really matter where your feet are – you could have one foot up on a rock, or you could be braced against a fast current while wading. Drop the tip of the rod down until it is touching the water, and pull in any slack over the right forefinger. Grip the right forefinger firmly to the cork, trapping the line against any risk of slipping while the cast is in progress.

The position of the left hand and arm are *critical*. Start by putting the left elbow against the left side of your waist *and keep it there*. If the left elbow migrates out in front of the waist during the backcast, the rod will go too far back (the equivalent of cocking the wrist with a single-handed rod) and the backcast will go too low.

Now point the left forearm at the target *and keep it pointed there*. If you do want to pull with the left hand on some casts, you cannot do it if the left hand is in front of your navel. With the left hand in front of your tummy you will end every cast in a hunched position, and after an hour your back will be killing you. It is essential that the left forearm remains pointing towards the target before and during the backcast. At a later stage, when you have grooved a good overhead cast into your muscle memory, you can relax the left arm a little and allow it to wander around, but during the learning stage, you should concentrate some of your attention on keeping the left forearm pointing at the target.

The movements of the right hand, and thus the rod, are the same as with a trout rod. Lift to 10 o'clock, flick back and up to 12.30, pause while the line flows out behind. The pause is usually longer, as the salmon cast tends to aerialise more line than does a trout cast, but with only 10 yards out of the rod tip (remember the AFTM scale and the rating of your rod to start with), the timing will be almost the same.

As soon as the line has completed its backwards flow through the air, push the right thumb out to full arm-stretch. This will involve the left hand in a movement from down beside your left waist to somewhere under your chin, but the movement is a following movement, not a driving movement. If the rod is going to be pointed out over the water as the right thumb drives it, the left hand, attached to the butt as it is, simply has to rise from its waist-high position to somewhere in front of the throat or chest.

While the line, fully extended, is falling gently onto the water, the arms are lowered back to their starting position. The overhead cast is complete.

Remember that the line goes fastest if it rolls over the top of the rod.

A recipe for a sore back. Holding the button of the rod in the left hand in front of the navel, commits you to bowing forwards on every forward cast.

By holding the left hand to the side of the waist, as shown here, a relaxed upright stance can be maintained all day. Notice how the left forearm points roughly at the target.

Thus the backcast and the forward cast must be in the same plane, even though the rod leans slightly to the right. There is a particularly common casting fault which I have come to call the 'Inverness Twitch', as I saw it first on the River Ness. The man who had this fault tried to tell me that he was doing a Spey cast, but he wasn't. The fault involves doing a little sideways switch of the rod tip as the backcast is coming back, so that the tip follows a curved path rearwards. The effect is to throw the backcast low and, as a consequence, the forward cast loses some of its power while the line is lifted over the top of the rod on its way forward. I showed this man that, by bringing the tip of the rod back and forth in the same plane he would gain about 5 yards in forward distance, and he went away muttering, as he had been taught to cast with this twitch by a casting school! Since then I have watched for this fault, and it does seem quite common among salmon anglers. There is, incidentally, one other penalty of the 'Inverness Twitch' and that is to twist the rod at the same time as it is bent in the backcast. Some makes of rod do not like this twist at all, and I have seen several of them break in the process, no doubt, because there were insufficient carbon fibres around the blank in proportion to the fibres running along the rod. This puts a terrific load on the resin which bonds the matrix together, because the fibres which resist the bending are no longer being stretched in a straight line on the outside of the curve of the rod – the fibres in a rod which is twisted are lying in a helix, and the spring loses a lot of its power in consequence.

All the faults enjoyed by the user of a single-handed rod are capable of being duplicated by the man wielding a salmon rod. Wind knots are still caused by too much effort. Hooks are broken by low backcasts, and low backcasts are caused by taking the rod too far back, either by sticking the left hand out or by stopping too much power too suddenly so that the tip flicks downwards before it comes to rest, or by leaving the backcast too long and allowing it to fall.

Shooting line is simplicity itself. After the rod has stopped at the end of the forward thrust, straighten the right forefinger and allow the line to shoot. It will all go tight, lying across the knuckles, and can be picked up by crooking the forefinger. Pull in line inboard of the forefinger and save yourself the excess energy involved in a constant reach with the left hand to the butt ring.

I said earlier that double-hauling is impossible with a salmon rod. It sometimes becomes necessary to cast a long, long way with a double-handed rod, and those who try it find that they have to aerialise a long line. By the time a long line has extended in the backcast, the bit near the tip ring will have started to drop and, however hard they try, they suffer a low backcast in consequence. Unless you want to fish with broken hooks, a long forward cast requires a high backcast, so that gravity is on your side, taking the line downhill to the target. There is a way of casting a very high backcast for maximum distance.

Start with the rod point down, touching the water. Start the power earlier, say at 9.30 instead of at 10 o'clock. As the backcast flick is done, raise the arms high at the same time, so that the rod stops, still pointing to 12.30, with the right arm fully extended above your head. You have thus

The start of the overhead cast with a salmon rod. As this cast is not intended to shoot any line, the line is trapped only by the little finger.

The lift is taken only to here, about 10 o'clock. Immediately this position is reached, and before the line has a chance to sag any more, the flick upwards and backwards is started.

applied the power of the backcast *upwards* as far as possible, but you have got yourself into a position where a good forward cast is impossible. Not only are the muscles which pull the right arm forward from up there much smaller than the muscles which punch from the shoulder, but, if you do start a forward cast with the right hand high, it can only track downwards. You are casting a long line, which requires a higher trajectory, so you should aim upwards.

It is essential that the elbows are dropped while the backcast is rolling out. Take care not to alter the position of the rod on its clock face. From a position at 12.30 above your head, the rod must be lowered to 12.30, with the right thumb beside your ear or in front of the ball of the right shoulder. From this position it is now possible to belt that right thumb out powerfully and, aiming above the horizontal, to throw the whole of a fly line straight out in front of you. You can shoot several yards of backing too, if you get the timing right (and if you are not overloading the rod by trying this trick with too heavy a fly line – safer to go to a line of one AFTM number lighter than the maker suggests for the rod). You are, after all, putting perhaps 25 yards of line up in the air, and that is over twice as much weight as the rod is designed to throw, assuming the AFTM numbers are the same for rod and line.

I have heard this dropping of the elbows likened to bringing the rod down through a tube. I have, however, found it easier to insist that the student thinks of his elbows and drops them so that the upper arms are approximately vertical. Or thinks of his right elbow and drops that – the left elbow will take care of itself.

For this cast to the limits of the rod and line, you will want to apply maximum power in the forward cast. For this the right arm alone is not enough, and a conscious effort should be made to pull inwards with the left hand towards the left side of the chest as the right thumb drives out and up. At the completion of the forward drive, the heel of the left hand is somewhere just in front of the left nipple and a female student, however buxom, will not hit herself with the rod provided that the right arm is fully extended.

Sometimes one wants to cast on the left side. Either the wind is blowing on to your right shoulder, or you are standing on the right bank, facing downstream, and there are trees to your right and behind you. You have a choice. If you are able to think ambidextrously, change hands and cast with the left hand uppermost on the rod. I cannot do this, and have never felt the need to concentrate on the necessary muscular discipline. Instead, I cross everything over, and cast my right thumb to my left ear. The left hand, of course, has now to be in front of the right-hand side of my waist. I have been told that it looks cack-handed, and on your first attempts, it will feel awkward, but it works for me, and for those strongly right-handed pupils I have taught to do it.

Casting into a wind is exactly the same as with a single-handed rod. Stop the backcast at 12 o'clock instead of 12.30 and the line will land into the teeth of a gale, dead straight.

Other casts, like the side cast, the slack line cast, the reach cast and the curve cast, can be done with a double-handed rod just as easily as with a

Notice how the upper right arm has hardly moved, and that the elbows stay low during the entire backcast. This shows the flick in progress.

The flick slowing down, all power finished. The line is rolling over the top of the rod, as the rod drifts slowly back while still keeping tension on the line in the air, so as to lengthen the available length of the stride of the forward cast.

The moment of truth. If everything is not set up correctly in the backcast, the forward cast cannot work. Right thumb no higher than the ear, left elbow still around the waist, so that the left hand is not stuck out. No shock waves in the line, and all rolled out straight, and at least as high as the tip of the rod.

A long smooth push with the right thumb will now throw a lovely straight forward cast like this, which hovers above the water for a split second before landing even a large fly gently.

117

To cast really long distances, a very high backcast is necessary. Starting with the tip touching the surface, the power of the flick is put in early (at 9.30 instead of at 10), and the whole rod thrown high. This delivers the backcast as high as possible, so that by the time it is all rolled out, it will still be as high as the rod tip in the next picture.
It is impossible to deliver much forward power from this position.

While the backcast is rolling out, the elbows are dropped downwards, without changing the angle of the rod. Thus the right thumb is brought to the ball of the right shoulder for maximum power in the forward drive. At the same time, the left hand pulls inwards towards the left waist, to further increase the power applied to the rod. Not a casting style to endure all day, but occasionally useful for casts of over 35 yards. Normally much more line would be shot than is shown in the photograph. The line is held under control but with no risk of tangles, simply by using the fingers of the hand highest up the handle.

single-handed rod. Provided that the weight of the big rod is taken in the left hand, the instructions given for the right hand, for any particular cast, can be followed.

19
THE DOUBLE-SPEY CAST

Every salmon angler has heard of the magic casts developed on the River Spey to cater for the high banks, overhanging trees and other obstructions found on this beautiful river. Evolved over many generations of highly skilled local anglers, the style of casting was, at one time, unique to this area. As the advantages of the Spey casts became more widely known, more and more anglers wanted to be able to do these casts, to the extent that, nowadays, there are special courses every year on the Spey, probably the best known being those run by Arthur Oglesby at Grantown on Spey. Arthur is President of the Association of Professional Game Angling Instructors, and a salmon angler of vast experience.

Spey casting has such a following on the river that many local anglers fish with no other style. Indeed I know a local ghillie whose Spey casting is poetry in motion, yet who confesses that he cannot do an overhead cast. Why should he deviate from Spey casting – he can cast the whole line out, and more, without running into problems of those overhanging branches which reach out and grab the flies of so many visiting anglers who are casting overhead?

There is an aura about Spey casting. A mystique has grown up around the style, to the point where the ordinary salmon angler, fishing in Scotland for a couple of weeks each year, develops a burning desire to be able to cast in this fashion. He hears that it is complicated, that one needs a special action in the rod, that it cannot be learned on grass or on stationary water. All very difficult. Fortunately, none of this is true.

However, when one stands on the bridge at Grantown and sees the local anglers fishing down the Association water, the rods seeming to sweep effortlessly back and forth and from side to side, and their lines sailing out over the river to huge distances, it is easy to forget that one is watching a succession of devoted anglers. Men who would rather fish than eat. Men who rush from work down to the river if the word goes round that the fish are in. Men who fish perhaps for four evenings a week and all day Saturday for several months of the year, and whose wives, born and bred of angling families, think that this is normal behaviour for a happily married man! Blessed are the anglers in that lovely part of the world, taught to fish by their fathers and other club members, and able to spend such a large part of their lives with a fly rod in their hands. Do something for long enough and to the onlooker it appears to be effortless. Watch a 50-year-old Spey angler, and you are seeing the product of 40 years of mis-spent eternal youth! Of course it looks easy.

Of the two casts, the single-Spey and the double-Spey, I find the double is the easier to master, so we shall discuss the double-Spey cast first, breaking it down into its component parts, each of which is simplicity itself. Put the simple parts together and you end up with a simple cast, and the mystery evaporates like the morning mist. If a student can roll cast, I can teach the double-Spey cast in a very short time, on running water, stillwater, or on grass.

The double-Spey cast, for a right-handed man, is the cast of choice if he is standing on the right bank of the river, facing downstream. It is also one of the safest casts if there is a strong downstream wind blowing – in this case you should have the right hand up the rod on the right bank, and the left hand up the rod on the left bank. The dedicated salmon angler should endeavour, therefore, to master roll casting with either hand at the top of the handle. If you are a holiday angler, content to go shopping with the family if the weather is really awful, you can get away with using only the right hand.

I find it easiest to teach the double-Spey cast by describing it as a roll cast with a wave of the rod before it. This sounds oversimple, perhaps, but that is all it is. Let us start by assuming that you are standing on the right bank, your line has fished around across the current, and is now lying straight downstream of you – on the dangle below you. There is one movement you can now make which will help to put a lot of fish in the bag, and which is not done by many anglers. Pull 1 or 2 yards of line in very slowly over your right forefinger, leaving 15 yards of line outside the tip ring.

The effect of this slow pull is to move the fly 1 or 2 yards straight upstream towards you. A fish may well be lying there, and will see the fly come across the current, hover for a moment, and then struggle away upstream against the current. The fish may well, in clear water, first see the fly do this when it is several yards upstream of its lie. Then you take a pace and fish out the next cast, and the fish sees the fly a yard nearer. Then another yard nearer. Then the next cast fishes the fly out to a position behind the fish's head, and the fly struggles up the current right over his nose. The temptation of this little struggling creature can often be more than the salmon can resist, and it will come up off its lie and take the fly. The angler feels the line tighten, and some may think they have hooked the bottom.

At this stage, the tyro angler will strike, a recipe for disaster. The fish has taken the fly in its mouth, and slowly, at the speed of the current, has sunk back to its lie, still facing the angler. A strike at this stage will either whip the fly out of the mouth of the fish, or hook it so lightly in the front of the mouth that it will come unstuck after a couple of thrashes on the surface. *Do not strike the fish on the dangle.*

What you should do is to let go the line you have pulled in over your forefinger, and wait for what will seem an agonising few seconds. When the line comes tight for the second time, lift the rod and start playing the fish, which will have been hooked by the drag of the current on line and

The double-Spey cast, as the beginner should start learning it. Do not, at this stage, try to shoot line. Start by sweeping the rod upstream, keeping the tip low.

Having put as much line to the left as possible, keeping the tip low, sweep the rod to the right.

As the rod sweeps to the right, notice that there is a knuckle in the line, being chased downstream.

As the rod comes around to a full arm-stretch to the right rear, the knuckle should be at least as far downstream as it is desired to deliver. The full arm-stretch is required to put as large a capital D of line behind and to the right as possible.

Then *drop the elbows* and, looking above your target . . .

. . . Belt out the delivery, aiming high – exactly as you would for a roll cast. Keep practising this style, and master it before you go on to the next stage. Notice that it is an essential part of the double-Spey that the leader and fly stay on the *downstream* side of the angler at all times. It is for this reason that the double-Spey is the cast of choice in a strong downstream wind – the fly stays downwind and cannot hit you!

123

leader from downstream of the fish's head. The hook will be embedded in the scissors at the corner of the mouth.

Sometimes, however, you will be lucky and the fish will take the fly and swim in a circle back to its lie. In this case there will be a great wrench on the line and the fish will be firmly hooked in the scissors with no action on the part of the angler. Perhaps one fish in ten will do this – the other nine will be lightly hooked, or missed altogether, if you strike on the dangle.

I talk a great deal while I am fishing, usually under my breath. I am talking to the fish, of course, not to myself. As I pull those two yards of line over my forefinger every time the fly comes onto the dangle, I say 'Come on, Fishy, Fishy', and anybody who hears me thinks I am suffering from senile decay. Perhaps I am, but I find that it helps me to think fish, and I was once told that the secret of successful salmon fishing is to think fish and to concentrate on what the fly is doing. By talking to the fish as I draw the line in, it helps me to draw slowly enough – do remember that a little shrimp or prawn, the size of your fly, would not be able to swim upstream against the current all that quickly. Make it look as if it was wounded and struggling, and you are more likely to appeal to the salmon's killer instinct. Here I must say that I do not wish to be drawn into an argument as to whether a salmon takes a fly out of a sense of killing, greed, hunger, annoyance, or anything else. All I will say is that I have caught a lot of fish while drawing the line in slowly on the dangle, which I do not think I would have caught if I had not drawn the line in.

You are now standing on the right bank, rod pointing down the river, and have 2 yards of line inboard of your right forefinger, and outboard of your right little finger. No fish has taken your fly, and you are ready to do the backcast of the double-Spey. This backcast is in two parts.

In order to learn the essential movements of the cast, I shall describe firstly how I teach it in an easily assimilated form, and then describe the variations, flicks and twitches which you can put in once you have built in muscle memory for the correct basic movements.

The first movement is to draw the tip ring slowly upstream to your left, as far as you can comfortably reach, keeping the tip ring within a foot of the water surface. This does two things. Firstly it puts some of the fly line upstream and to your left, and secondly it draws the fly upstream towards you, skating it on the surface (unless it is very heavy indeed). The fly must not leave the water at this stage. The moment you reach full arm-stretch to the left, dump the 2 yards of slack line off your forefinger by just straightening the finger and then re-gripping the rod with it.

The second movement starts by dropping the tip ring to within 3 or 4 inches of the water and sweeping the rod round to your right. As the tip ring travels over the surface, the line is pulled out through the rings by surface tension. If the tip is not within a couple of inches of the water the line will not pull out through the rings. Keep the rod coming around to the right, and as you do so you will see in the line in front of you on the surface, an angle being chased downstream – I have heard it described as a knuckle in the line caused by folding the line back on itself. By the time this little right angle in the line on the water reaches a position, perhaps 45° downstream from your feet, the rod should be round to your right, behind

Taken from above, this series shows the next stage in learning for the beginner – shooting line. Here the rod is swept as far to the left as possible. The line to be shot is held under the forefinger. As soon as this position is reached, the line is dumped by straightening the forefinger.

As the rod sweeps back to the right, the line is dragged out through the rings. In this photograph the line is just starting to shoot.

Here the rod is well around to the right, and the line is shooting. Because the whole cast is being speeded up (but still not rushed) and the photograph is taken from above, the knuckle appears larger.

The belly swayed around to the right rear, arms still extended into the reach around. The whole of the shoot is completed, resulting in the capital D of line containing 2 yards more line than would have been the case if no shoot had taken place. With a bigger capital D, the delivery will go farther.

Showing how the elbows are dropped, with the rod leaning slightly to the right. (This is a different cast from the previous photo, and the line is nearer the angler's legs – but still safe.)

The delivery is made forwards and high and, as the line lands, the arms are relaxed inwards and the rod tip dropped to within a foot of the surface. All set now to fish the cast around, take a pace, and enjoy the next poetry-in-motion double-Spey cast.

you, and your arms should be stretched up and to your right. You will find that you have turned from the waist, and your shoulders are now facing almost downstream.

The line, meanwhile, will have formed a big belly behind you and to your right, and you should have laid the bottom of the capital D on the water or the bank about half a rod-length to the right of your feet. *Now drop your elbows*, and check that the rod is at 2 o'clock; both of these actions are essential to the correct delivery of the forward cast.

If you do not drop your elbows, your right thumb, and thus the rod tip, will track downwards in the forward delivery, instead of outwards. If you do not check that the rod is set up at 2 o'clock, you will have no control over the height of the forward cast. If at this stage you are still puzzled, go back and read Chapter 16 on roll casting and all will become clear.

The forward cast is exactly the same, and I mean exactly the same, as the forward cast of the roll cast. Belt the right thumb out to a point slightly higher than horizontal and to full arm-stretch. As the line is extended and starting to fall, lower your arms and relax. You have just done your first correct double-Spey cast. You will notice that you shot some line – the line you had drawn in on the dangle. You did not shoot it on the delivery, however; you shot it into the backcast. By doing this you made the belly of line behind you larger than it would otherwise have been, and a rule of the roll cast is that the larger the belly behind you, the better the forward delivery will go. I must stress that I did not invent this move. I was first shown the trick by Kenny Jack, a boatman on the Tweed, who had seen an angler doing it and had admired his style. The angler turned out to be Major Ashley-Cooper, one of the great salmon anglers of all time. Shooting line into the backcast of the roll cast or the double-Spey will add several yards to the forward cast, without the penalty of any extra effort. It is just a more efficient way of doing it, and very much more effective than trying to shoot line on the forward delivery.

The whole of the double-Spey cast is carried out without a pause. Constant sweeping gentle movements are the key to greater distance and less fatigue. You can take your time over the first sweep, that to the left, providing the fly is made to skate on the surface. Do not hurry this move, or the fly will be lifted from the water and may go to the left, or upstream, side of you, and if you try to deliver a forward cast with the fly in this position it will whip back and embed itself in your person. It is essential that the fly stays on the water, and downstream of your feet, right up until the moment it is picked up and carried out by the forward roll of the line.

It is also essential that the line is laid a few feet to your right when the belly behind you is formed, and that the rod is leaning to your right as you drop your elbows and check the set-up is at 2 o'clock. It is a recipe for the fly sticking in you if the rod is brought upright, or swept behind the right shoulder too far, because, when the forward cast is done, and the fly starts by coming backwards, it will again stick in you. Bad idea, particularly if you are using an Esmond Drury treble, and all three points puncture you!

If you find there is some loose line inboard of the butt ring after you have formed the belly behind and to the right, stop and capture it under the forefinger. Loose line will leach away much of the power of the forward cast.

How to add the little flips which allow for much greater distances being cast. Start by having perhaps 3 yards of shooting line (once you are really good you can manage perhaps 7 or 8 yards!) trapped under the forefinger. Reach as far to the left as possible.

Dump the line off the forefinger, and *flip* the cast back to the right.

With a sweeping flip of the rod tip, chase the knuckle swiftly to the right . . .

. . . And put as large a belly of line behind you as you can. The larger the better, providing that the fly is still downstream of you. If you overdo this part of the cast, the fly will be driven back at you.

Now drop the right elbow in towards the body and drive a powerful thrust of the right thumb forwards and upwards.

The cast sails away over the surface – to land lightly. The arrow shows where the knuckle was at the moment the forward cast started. If the belly is on the right, because the cast was done with the right hand up the rod, the delivery must be to the left of the knuckle on the water. Failure to observe this rule will result in the line crossing itself and tangling.

With really huge amounts of line, some people advocate throwing lots of line to the left. In doing this, all of the line leaves the water and lands again, but it is still *essential* that the fly stays downstream of the angler. The arrow shows the position of the fly as it lands after the first movement. No line is being shot in this photograph.

Showing how the forward cast, whether it be a roll, double-Spey or single-Spey, should be aimed high and forwards, to full arm-stretch. Power applied over a longer time is more total power, so keep that forward thrust going until you run out of arm! One of the commonest mistakes made by beginners is that they do not aim high enough.

We have now completed the description of the basic movements of the double-Spey, and you should practise these until you have built in muscle memory for them all. You may find, however, that your casting lacks the smooth flowing style you have so admired while leaning on that bridge at Grantown, and there is a reason. The men you see casting there are using a lot of line – probably the whole of a 35- or 40-yard line.

It is time for you to cast farther, and in so doing you will be able to develop style and rhythm. Do not forget the basic principles, but use them with a longer stride, so to speak, and do the cast in waltz time.

Start from our original position, line below you on the dangle, 2 yards of line in over the forefinger, feet firmly set on the river bed or bank, your whole body and legs facing downstream and across, say at 45° downstream, to where you want the fly to land. You now have 20 yards of line outside the tip ring. Do not think you are going to cast only 20 yards, as you have 5 yards of rod, 3 yards of leader, and you are going to shoot 2 yards, so the fly should land 30 yards away from your feet, and that is a hell of a distance in anyone's language!

The leftwards, upstream, movement of the rod can now contain a little flick of the rod tip in a rising arc. This will perhaps lift all the line off the water as it comes upstream, but the fly *must* be dumped downstream of your feet. Remember safety, and if you overdid the little flick, and the fly landed upstream of you, allow the current to carry it below you before you make another move.

The split second the rod stops, dump the trapped line from under your forefinger, and start the sweep to the right rear. Again put a little flick, or switch, into the tip of the rod, and you will throw a larger belly of line (capital D) behind and to your right. The bottom of the D must still be only a few feet from your legs, and you must still drop your elbows and check the set-up at 2 o'clock. You will find that the line will shoot out through the rings, this time because of the inertia of the greater length of line being swept back – the rod tip can sweep back at head height or above, and the more line you have out the higher will that sweep have to be. Leave the rod leaning slightly to your right, so that the tip ring is vertically over the line lying on the bottom of the D.

Now belt the line out high in front of you and watch with great satisfaction how it unrolls *above the surface*, hovers for a moment, and lands gently. You have now put the final polish on your double-Spey cast. And you thought it was difficult?

You can now get the final plaudit from your friends by imagining that you are fishing the left bank, with a strong downstream wind. Change hands, left hand up the rod and doing the work, and practise the double-Spey. Master that one, and you can, almost, call yourself an accomplished caster with a double-handed rod.

20
THE SINGLE-SPEY CAST

The final touch of craftsmanship for the salmon angler, and the most difficult to learn, is the single-Spey cast. I think it is the most difficult because it is all done in one continuous motion. Stop anywhere and it all goes wrong. For this reason it is essential to get each of the four parts right in turn, adding on bits until the whole cast is mastered.

In years gone by, people used to call the single-Spey cast a 'switch' cast. There is a basic difference between the switch and the single-Spey, which results in the single-Spey cast going a few yards farther. I shall cover that little difference later.

If you are strongly right-hand-oriented, as I am, you will find yourself wanting to do all your casting with the right hand up the rod. On the left bank, therefore, the single-Spey is the cast to use.

In a strong upstream wind, the single-Spey cast should be used off both banks, changing hands to use the left hand up the rod on the right bank. The reason is safety, as the single-Spey takes the fly upstream of you, and thus downwind – and however hard the wind is blowing, you cannot get the fly stuck in you.

Start by standing on the left bank of the river (or on a stillwater, facing along the shore to your left, or on a grass field, with an imaginary river flowing right to left). Place your feet, for preference, facing your target, roughly 45° across and down. Turn your shoulders to face the line, which is on the dangle downstream of you, and with about 10 yards of line outside the rod tip after you have talked to the fish and drawn in those vital couple of yards. You are now all set to do a single-Spey cast.

There are four distinct parts to a single-Spey, they form one long continuous movement when added together, but we must consider them one by one, and you must master each one in turn, then add it to the preceding parts. Only when you have mastered all four parts will the cast go right:

The lift

The line is downstream of you on the dangle. What you have to do is to get as much of it off the water as possible. If you are fishing a sinking line, it often helps to do a roll cast along the shore to bring the line to the surface. With a fast current, the lift will do this anyway, because the current gets under the line and brings it up as the line is tightened in the lift, but with a deeply sunk line it is advisable to roll it as a preliminary stage.

Starting with the rod tip low, do a slow steady lift of the rod and the arms to lift as much line off the water as you can. Do not lift the rod above the 10.30 position. Keep the line tight and feel as if you were in control of it. Some people advise lifting inshore, with the rod tip angling to your left so that, at the completion of the lift, the rod tip is inshore of your left shoulder. Frankly, while I can quite see that this helps throw the line in the desired direction in the next move, I am concerned that it also brings the fly too near to one's person, and thus I prefer to teach a straight lift, with the rod tip coming up absolutely vertically, so that the rod tip tracks up and back in the same plane as the line is lying. The split second the rod tip reaches 10.30, you start . . .

The switch

This is the tricky part of the single-Spey. It is also the most difficult part to describe. One way is to say that you look at the rod tip, and with it draw a rising crescent, starting with a horizontal line and ending with an upwards flick. The other way is to look at the fly, and move the rod tip so that all the line is picked up and switched to your right rear, turning from the waist slightly as you do so. (When this switch is completed, your shoulders should be facing your target, 45° across the river). Yet another description is that the fly and leader are flicked outboard and upstream, so that the fly lands on the water one rod-length outboard of you, and at least one rod-length upstream of you. Note that the last movement is an *upwards* flick of the rod tip, to keep as much of the line as possible in the air.

It is at this point that the difference between the switch cast and the single-Spey cast becomes apparent. In the switch cast, the fly does not touch the water. In the single-Spey cast the fly and leader are quite deliberately kissed onto the surface upstream of your feet. Surface tension will grip them, so that, on the delivery, the spring of the rod is cocked more, and throws the line with more power. In this manner, the single-Spey will outdistance the switch by several yards.

I once saw Lefty Kreh give a masterly demonstration of casting at the Chatsworth Angling Fair, and he described this kiss of the fly on the water as a 'water haul', attributing extra distance to the fact that there was extra resistance, thus extra cocking of the spring of the rod. He was using a single-handed rod, of course, but the principle is the same.

The power required for the switch is very little. All you are doing is picking 10 yards of line off the water downstream of you, and gently switching it upstream so that the tail end of it kisses the surface 5 yards upstream of you. If you omit the little upwards twitch at the end of the movement, too much line will land on the water, and much of the energy of the forward cast will be wasted in unsticking it from that surface tension. If you do not switch hard enough, the fly will not go upstream of you. If this happens – *freeze* – do not do the forward cast or you will get a fly stuck in you. Roll the line forward, downstream, and start all over again.

Remember that this is the cast of choice in a strong *upstream* wind. Keep that fly outboard of you, over the river, and put it behind you, upstream and downwind. That is the only safe place for it to go.

Having done the switch upstream and upwards, and while the line is travelling into the backcast, you must carry out the third stage of the cast.

The start of the single-Spey. The rod lifted high, pointing straight downstream. Lift as much line off the water as possible.

Some people lift the rod up, leaning slightly to the left, inboard of the line of dangle . . . This makes little difference, but it does drive the fly closer to the body on the next move, and is thus slightly less safe.

Side view, showing how the rod is lifted high, at full arm-stretch.

The drop

As soon as the switching movement is complete, you will be standing facing downstream at 45°, with your arms extended upstream. Actually your right arm should be upstream at 45°, and pointing skywards at 45°. At this stage you must *drop your elbows*. Sounds familiar, doesn't it? For the same reason as I have mentioned it often before, you want to deliver forwards and upwards to give the line a trajectory to fall in while it is being delivered to the target. You cannot aim upwards if the right thumb starts off higher than your ear, so by dropping the elbows you set yourself up for the forwards and upwards delivery. The elbows must complete their drop quite quickly, so that they are low by the time the fly kisses down upstream of you. In other words the elbows are being dropped after the switch of the rod tip is complete, but while the line is still travelling upstream. Keep your eye on the fly, and as soon as it kisses, deliver . . .

The forward cast

Basically this is exactly the same as the delivery of the roll cast and the single-Spey. You drive the right thumb outwards and upwards above your target area. If you are casting a very long line, you pull with the left hand as well but to start with, concentrate on just the right hand and forget the left. If the line crashes onto the water a few yards away, you forgot to drop your elbows.

The split second the rod tip stops at the end of the forward thrust, shoot those 2 yards of line by straightening the forefinger. Here again is a difference to remember – shoot line on the forward cast in a single-Spey, but into the backcast of the double-Spey, remember?

*   *   *

That completes the description of the basic moves. Get any one of them wrong and the whole cast will be wrong. Get them all correct, and the cast will rocket out over the river, landing lightly, and you will grin with satisfaction.

Practise with a shortish line to start with. Keep casting, analysing your faults as you do so, and correcting them as soon as you identify what went wrong. Only when you have mastered the single-Spey with 10 yards outside the rod tip should you start to increase the distance.

For greater distance, the rod must start right down on the surface. Lift slightly less, say to 10 o'clock, so that the switch can be put in earlier, and thus to a higher aiming point behind to allow a greater length of line to extend before it drops. Kiss the fly farther upstream, say three or four rod-lengths, but still only one rod-length outboard of your feet. Because you have more line travelling backwards you will have a slightly longer time in which to drop the elbows. The right thumb must start the forward cast no higher than the ball of the right shoulder. Aim higher on the forward delivery. Because you have more line travelling fast outside the tip ring, you will be able to shoot more line.

The switch well in progress. The right arm is still extended, and the line travelling upstream, well outboard of the angler.

The movement of the rod completed as the switching action stops. The line is still travelling upstream, passing the angler at least a rod-length away from his body. While the line is still moving, you must
. . .

. . . Drop the elbows. Failure to drop the elbows is why so many anglers have difficulty with the single-Spey. Notice that the fly and leader are kissing the water at this moment, but that the whole of the line is still in the air. The elbows must be dropped before the fly touches the water, so that as soon as the fly is seen to kiss, the forward cast can start. This photo is deceptive – the belly of line is no nearer the bank than the angler.

The forward cast, aimed high, punching a nice streamlined loop out over the water. Notice that the forward cast is carried out to full arm-stretch. Power applied over a longer time is more total power. Push with the right thumb until you run out of arm.

Side view of the fly coming off the water as the forward cast is delivered. If this was a student, my instant comment would be that he or she had aimed too low, as my right thumb should be at eye level!

A common fault in the single-Spey. Dump too much line on the water in the switch and you will hear it tearing off as you deliver. This soaks up much of the power of the forward cast, and costs you distance.

Watch a real expert lifting and switching the whole of a fly line, and shooting up to 10 yards of backing, and you will realise that a bit of studied practice is required to achieve that standard!

Now for a quick summary of some of the faults in a single-Spey, and how to spot them. If you lift too fast and stop, the line will sag, and the switch will not be a clean pick-up, but will be jerky. If you switch too hard, the fly will not go to its correct touch-down position of one rod-length outboard and at least one rod-length upstream, and may not kiss on the surface. If the fly does not kiss, you cut the forward distance by yards. If you switch too far round to your right, the line will catch on the bank upstream of you –remember everything must happen outboard of the rod tip. If the fly smacks you on the right shoulder as you deliver, you brought the rod too upright while you were dropping your elbows – remember to leave it leaning to your right, so that the tip ring is as far as possible vertically over the line to which it will give the forward power. If you hear a tearing noise as you cast forward, you have put too much of the line on to the water, and you are wasting the power of the forward cast in unsticking the excess line – aim to kiss only the fly and the leader. If the line crashes on to the water in front of you, I will say it once more, you forgot to lower your elbows. . . . I have found this to be the most common mistake by those who fail to execute a single-Spey cast as nicely as they would wish.

You will experience poetry in motion, all one smooth succession of moves, and almost a sensuous pleasure when you get into the rhythm of single-Spey casting. It feels great, and it allows you to fish safely and in places impossible with other casts.

The commonest fault in the single-Spey. Failure to drop the elbows means that the forward cast starts with the arms held high at the completion of the switch. The right thumb thus has no choice but to track downwards. The delivery goes downwards, hitting the water very hard and before being fully extended. Crashing the line on to the surface, as in this photograph, scares the living daylights out of fish and causes them to stop eating . . . so they will not take your fly!

21
SALMON ON A SHOOTING HEAD

Anglers these days crave for distance in their casting. Frequently it is not necessary, but there is a school of thought in salmon fishing which believes that a long cast downstream instead of a short one will put more fish in the bag. The reasoning goes something like this. A long line will result in the fly swimming more slowly over the fish, and this is true. The farther away from a lie that your size 10 boots are crunching on the gravel underwater, the less likely are the fish to be disturbed or frightened, and this is also true. In theory, therefore, there are two very good reasons for casting a long line with a salmon rod.

But how long is a long line? On small rivers, and there are many well-known salmon rivers in Scotland which are only 10 or 15 yards wide, a cast of 25 yards would be regarded as a long cast. On large rivers like the Tay and the Tweed, which are over 50 yards wide in places, a very much longer cast is seen by some anglers to be needed for best results.

I am well aware that the speed of the fly over the bottom is not governed by the length of the cast, but by the angle, relative to the current, to which the fly is cast, and whether line is mended during the swim of the fly. By wading in well above the fish and casting more downstream, the fly is made to swim slowly. By casting straight across, the fly will swim faster. So, in theory it is possible, by positioning yourself directly upstream of a fish, to make the fly swim so slowly that it is stationary relative to the bottom – some people call this 'dapping' or 'dibbling', or 'dangling' the fly, and a very seductive method it can be, particularly if a long hair-winged fly like a Collie Dog is skated at the neck of a pool. The problem is that, unless one is sitting on a rock, the fish will smell you.

I am convinced that salmon do have a very keen sense of smell. It is, after all, believed that they detect their home river by smelling the water in the estuary, or even well out to sea. I do not believe, therefore, that it is a good idea to dunk your waders into the water immediately upstream from a creature which has such a keen sense of smell and/or taste. The corollary would be the deer stalker who positions himself directly upwind of a deer and expects it to stand still – it will usually bolt at the first whiff of a human being. Why should salmon not do the same? There would appear to be, therefore, a prejudice against deep wading and short casting, in favour of shallow wading (or no wading at all) and long casting.

In recent years there has therefore developed a school of salmon fly anglers who use shooting heads in order to achieve greater distances. The use of a shooting head on a double-handed rod carries with it some problems not met by the trout fisherman.

To cast a shooting head, in particular to roll cast a shooting head, requires that the rear end of the head is positioned near the tip ring. In technical terms you have very little overhang; overhang being the length of monofilament or braided shooting line outside the tip ring. Let us assume you have cast 45 yards, and the fly has swum around onto the dangle downstream of you. Let us also assume that you have a 12-yard head, a 5-yard rod and a 3-yard leader. In order to make the next cast, you will have to pull in 24 yards of monofilament to allow only 1 yard of overhang. What on earth are you going to do with it all?

Casting this distance with a full dressed double-taper line would not present nearly the same problem, as you would probably aerialise 25 yards, and shoot 15 yards (the rod's 5 yards of length making up the difference). Assuming also that this length of cast is usually only made with a 40-yard dressed line, there will only be 5 yards of backing and 10 yards of fly line to hold in loops over the forefinger and shoot on the delivery – no great problem. 24 yards of monofilament is an altogether different matter, and the tangles can be horrific.

Even if the whole of the 24 yards is drawn in and allowed to fall onto the surface of the water, it will be carried off downstream in the current. By the time the cast is made, there will be a long loop trailing away, which will soak up a considerable amount of power as it is dragged off the surface back towards the butt ring in the shoot. Distance suffers in consequence.

A very good friend of mine, who says he would prefer to remain anonymous, came up with the idea of using a fixed spool reel instead of a normal fly reel. The shooting head has a loop on the end, and is normally stored separately from the reel and its monofilament. At the beginning of the day the line is threaded through the rings, and the monofilament tied securely to the loop on the shooting head.

Line is allowed to pay out until there is 1 yard of overhang, then the bail arm is flipped back and the forefinger of the left hand traps the monofilament against the spool. The right forefinger also traps the monofilament against the cork. The cast is made and, as the rod stops, both forefingers are straightened and out flies the line, paying off sweetly from the fixed spool reel. As the fly and line land, the reel handle is clicked over to engage the bail-arm pick-up, perhaps a couple of turns to remove any slack in the line, and the fly is fished around as normal. When the fly reaches the end of its travel and is on the dangle, the reel is slowly wound to bring the fly up-current until there is only 1 yard of overhang. Then the pace is taken and the whole process repeated.

The advantages of this method are legion. There is no risk of tangles. The line shoots farther. The line is under greater control. When a fish is hooked, the line can be wound in more quickly than with a fly reel, and there is a slipping clutch to help in avoiding breaks. Marvellously simple, and my friend wonders why it hasn't been thought of before. Who knows, perhaps it has...?

Before you go and hunt out a fixed spool reel to use with your shooting head, I would earnestly entreat you to check the rules, written and unwritten, of the water you intend to fish in this manner. There are people who believe that a fly on the end of a line is not the only requirement for fly fishing, and recent rule suggestions for the beats on the River Tweed are a case in point. I hear that the use of a shooting head is to be banned on this river because of its common use in snatching. There are those who disapprove of the use of a fixed spool reel, and, if they own the water, or make the rules, you have no choice but to stick to traditional methods.

Before the average angler rushes off for pen and paper to tell me that I am exaggerating by talking about casts of 45 yards being normal, may I assure you that there are many anglers on the River Tay who habitually cast 45 to 50 yards with a shooting head. I have heard from a most reliable source of a man who usually casts 60 yards, but I have to admit that he is using an 18-foot powerhouse of a rod. As far as I am aware, only 18-foot rods made by Hardy's of Alnwick are capable of this huge distance – I have paced 56 yards with my own 15-footer, and I nearly bust a gut to do it. I certainly could not fish at that level of effort for very long, and even a few demonstration casts with a big rod and a shooting head made from 12 yards of a DT 12 fast-sinking line will sort out the men from the boys. If your breakfast was only a cup of tea and a cigarette you certainly won't be able to do it!

22

AFTER THE LINE HAS LANDED

Logically a book on casting should stop at the moment the line lands! However it is an essential part of fishing that we also discuss the control of the line after you have put it out on the water.

This chapter applies to the stillwater angler from the bank and from a boat, as much as to the river fisherman, although it is mainly on rivers that problems of line control become most apparent. If I confine my discourse to the river situation, the reservoir angler can pick from it what he needs.

When casting a line across a current, the straightness of the line is a transient thing. The current will soon form a belly in the line, causing the fly to be dragged faster and faster until it eventually ends up below the angler, pointing straight down the current – on the dangle.

There are occasions when one wants the fly to behave thus. Some trout seem to be triggered into a take by a fly whipping past their noses – almost as if it is food that will get away unless they grab at it. Occasionally in salmon fishing, too, a fast-moving fly is taken when a sedate offering has been ignored time and time again. Funny things, fish, they do not seem to think the same way as we do! The key to successful fishing therefore seems to be to ring the changes until the desired effect is achieved and the fish succumbs to temptation.

Much control over the fly's movements can, of course, be given by the rod tip, either by following the line around or by leading the line. The rod which holds back on the line will make the fly move at a different speed, and over a different track through the water, than will a rod which is swung around before the line pulls it.

Even more control can be exercised over the line by moving it in a positive way after it has landed on the water, to give it a belly, or curve. If the line is a sinker, this movement must be carried out immediately it lands on the surface and before it has time to sink. Once sunk, almost nothing can be done. Floating lines can be moved around almost at will during the whole time they are lying on the surface. This movement is generally called 'mending the line'.

Mending the line is very easy. Little girls do it when they are twirling a skipping rope, and you do it when the garden hose catches on a stone in the rockery, so why should you not be able to do it with a fishing rod in your hand?

Twirl the rod tip in a circle. Draw an 'O' with the tip ring. Flick the line upwards and to one side. These expressions are all used to describe how to mend line. The shorter the rod, the more positive the movement at the handle has to be. With a salmon rod, the tip ring describes a circle, the diameter of which can be as much as 6 feet, and is a more leisurely action than is needed to mend line with a short trout rod – this has to be a sharper flicking movement.

To mend line, a double-taper or a single-taper line, is needed. Mending line is almost impossible with a weight-forward, and totally impossible with a shooting head.

While the tip ring is swirling around, some drag at the fly is inevitable unless some slack line is fed under the right forefinger as the swirl takes place. With a dry fly, failure to shoot a little line as the mend is made almost always results in the fly being drowned.

It pays not to become hidebound in one's approach, and the mend, while usually done in an upstream direction to slow the fly's swim, can also be done downstream to speed up the track of the fly. Variety is the key, until you catch a fish. Then you know what that particular fish wanted. The next one might want something entirely different!

There is one other form of line movement. I do not think it has a name, but the wet fly angler, gently dibbing his rod tip up and down as the fly swims round, is imparting a little twitch to the passage of the fly, making it look as if it is swimming in little jerks. Studying nymphs in my aquarium some years ago, I have seen them swim in these little short dashes with a rest between, and I have also seen them swimming in a straight purposeful path from one weedbed to another, so I cannot say that one swimming style is more realistic than another. What I do know is that a wet fly, or a salmon fly, cast across and down and held on a tight line until it is on the dangle, has swum the equivalent of an Olympic marathon, faster and faster, and that I have never seen nymphs or shrimps do that.

While this twitching of the rod tip as the fly swims around is common amongst wet fly anglers, I wonder why the salmon angler is seen doing it so seldom? Don't little creatures in the sea swim with pauses in between each dash? Food for thought?

The last form of line movement I would like to mention is no movement at all. I was once fishing the lovely River Alness in baking hot weather. A family on one of the beats consisted of Dad, who was a relatively experienced angler, Mum, who had fished occasionally, and two boys of about 8–10 years old. It was suggested that the two boys should sit on a rock at the head of a pool, holding a fly rod, and dibble the fly in the fast water. A Collie Dog was tied onto two strong leaders, and the boys were shown how to hold the rods out over the neck of the pool. The flies skated around for what seemed ages. Fish jumped over the leaders, splashing the two boys. The sun seemed to get hotter and hotter, and one of the boys decided to go and explore the glen. The younger one stayed, sitting like a graven image on his rock.

Suddenly there was a great slosh, the reel screamed, the rod bent, and he had a fish on. Why did that salmon take that fly, presumably after eyeing it skating around in the white water above him for over an hour? We shall never know, but that was one very happy small boy, who caught the only fish of the day, and he knew absolutely nothing about casting!

23
LOOP CONTROL

So far in the book I have endeavoured to make everything easy to read, easy to understand, and thus easy to follow and execute. There is a reason for my not being too technical.

A couple of years ago, I had a casting lesson booked by a man's secretary, and the phone call was followed by a confirmation letter on company notepaper, where not only the time was confirmed, but also the duration of the lesson, and the cost! All very efficient, and I was curious to see what sort of hot-shot captain of industry would turn up. At the appointed minute, a very large car scattered gravel in the driveway, being steered with one hand by a man who was holding his car telephone in the other. As he opened the door, a blast of cold air hit me, and I realised that the car was air-conditioned, unusual in the UK. Despite the low temperature in the car, the man had a sheen of perspiration on his forehead, and he leapt out of the car and shook my hand. 'Right', he said, 'Let's get on with it. I am going fishing next week with some customers, and you have got one hour to teach me. I don't want you to blind me with theory, just show me what to do and I will do it!' And he did exactly that, bless him. In that hour, I had only to show him anything once, and he copied it perfectly. I complimented him on his total coordination, but then suggested that he should slow down, or he would get ulcers and a heart attack. He told me he had the ulcers, and the heart attack was a risk associated with his lifestyle. As he drove out of the drive, scattering gravel again, he had the telephone in his hand.

I do not tell this story just to illustrate that the poor man was perhaps going to kill himself in his ambition to be the richest customer-entertaining angler in the country. What stuck in my mind was that he followed my movements exactly, and the casting went beautifully. He did not understand one word of the theory. He couldn't care less about the theory. 'Don't confuse me with facts – just show me what to do.' And it worked – for him. So in writing this book, I have adopted the same tack. I have shown you what to do. I have explained what causes things to go wrong. But I have not gone too deeply into the theory. It is time now to do so, for the benefit of those readers who, having learned to cast, are prepared to run the risk of being bamboozled by the theory. Let me assure you that you will not need a doctorate in physics to understand what follows.

A fly line is a long thin flexible weight. Its weight is governed by the AFTM scale. Its length is governed by you, as we are concerned only with the length outside the tip ring (and down the rod, as this does affect the spring of the rod to a degree, but for the purpose of our discussions it can be ignored). The flexibility is governed by the manufacturer who opted for a certain mixture of core material and of coating material (in which may be additives like air bubbles, glass bubbles, or lead powder, all designed to give positive or negative buoyancy). The flexibility can also be governed by ambient temperature, or by the temperature of the water. A great deal of research is carried out by line manufacturers to get the correct balance of properties for the angler. I shall return to this in Chapter 24.

Any weight is affected by the laws of physics. It will have inertia – that property by which, when at rest, it tends to remain so, resisting movement. Once moving, it will have momentum – the product of its mass multiplied by its velocity. It will be affected by wind resistance – being slowed down by the density of the air through which it is moving. Wind resistance increases with the square of the velocity – so a line moving twice as fast will have four times the wind resistance to overcome. And lastly it will be affected by gravity.

For maximum distance in casting, therefore, the line has to have its inertia overcome, and then be given maximum velocity combined with minimum wind resistance, with an allowance for gravity. Simple, isn't it, or are your eyes glazing over already?

Inertia is complicated by the fact that, in fishing, we are lifting the line off the water. Surface tension will add to the inertia, making the line more resistant to the initial movement. For this reason the angler starting a cast by just snatching the rod back will find that his backcast does not go as far, or as nicely, as it should, because much of the power he thought he was putting into the backcast is being soaked up in overcoming inertia and surface tension. Once the line actually gets moving through the air, not enough power is left to drive it in a nice flowing backcast. Inertia and surface tension are overcome in the initial lift of the rod, and will, to a certain extent, cause the spring of the rod to be cocked a little. If, at this stage, the rod stops, even momentarily, the line will sag, inertia and surface tension will re-exert themselves, and he will have to start all over again to overcome them. So, once started in movement of the backcast, don't stop, but accelerate the tip of the rod upwards and backwards to give the line its velocity into the backcast. The actual velocity will be dictated by the power of the spring, the amount of effort you put into cocking it, and whether you allow the spring to uncock at the correct moment, and without interference with the direction of rod tip.

How much effort you put into the cast is up to you, but it should be only that which is needed to put the line high and straight. Any extra is only wasted calories – it will burn up your breakfast and contribute to the Greenhouse Effect.

The power of the spring is dictated by the blank manufacturer. A strong spring obviously will require more power from you to cock it, but it will throw a heavier weight at the desired speed than a softer spring. The blank maker usually rates his rod to show you the correct AFTM number for that rod, and that is a simple way of telling you how many grams of line you should hang on the end of the spring. Aerialise more line than the suggested 10 yards, and you increase the weight and decrease the ability of the rod spring to deliver velocity. It can be self-defeating to aerialise more line in order to cast farther because, by losing velocity, you lose momentum, and momentum is what overcomes wind resistance.

It is, of course, perfectly possible to maintain momentum, even with more weight hung on the tip, by forcing the spring to deliver more power by putting in more power yourself in the first place. But there is a practical limit to your muscle power, and how long you can cast before you turn into a jellied wreck. We are, after all, talking about the sort of casting you can maintain for a whole fishing day.

Allowing the spring to uncock at the correct moment results in the line being thrown in the required direction. If the spring uncocks at the wrong moment, the line will go in the wrong direction. We have already discussed the desirability of throwing the line high behind you, so that its forward track is downhill. The moment the tip ring starts to move back past 12 o'clock it is tracking in a downwards curve, throwing the line lower than it should be. A little allowance of half an hour to 12.30 is permissible (unless you are casting into a wind, see Chapter 6) but any power further back than 12.30 will cost you distance in the forward cast, or broken hooks behind on the ground.

Up until this moment, the line has been pulled under tension by the rod tip. The momentum given to the line by this pulling action will cause the line to keep going backwards after the rod tip stops. One end of the weight, however, is held back by the tip ring (or by tension in the line down through the rings) and, as the tip stops, the line starts to roll over the end of the rod, forming the loop. At that stage, all the power you can give to the line has already been given, and the line is committed on its path through the air. You cannot now make it go any faster than it is already moving.

Interference with the direction in which the line has been thrown can come about by allowing the tip to vibrate. One end of the weight is virtually fixed to the tip ring and, if the tip vibrates, a wave effect is sent along the line. This disturbs the smooth flow of power, and the commonest effect is the tailing loop, and the resultant wind knots.

Wind resistance is proportional to the frontal area of the object travelling through the air, assuming that the velocity is constant. The frontal area of a fly line is made up of two components as it flies through the air – the width of the line, and the length of it which is presented to the air. There is also a drag component dependent upon the roughness of the surface, but this can be ignored.

The frontal area of the rolling loop is the key. Nothing can be done about the width component, as this is the fatness or slimness built in by the manufacturer. For a given weight, a floater will be bulkier, and have more wind resistance, than a sinker, which is why all distance casting competitors use sinkers. The length component is dependent upon the shape of the loop. A tight loop will be more streamlined than will a wide loop.

The more streamlined the shape of the loop, the farther will it go for a given amount of effort. In other words – the more streamlined the loop, the less effort will it require to cast a given distance.

So the key to maximum distance for minimum effort lies in loop control. Loop control is an expression used frequently by those who write articles in fishing magazines, and almost always they are talking only about the forward cast. Loop control is just as important in the backcast, as energy is often expended wastefully in the backcast. Those writers who tell you to time the forward cast by waiting for the tug of the line at the back are among those who waste energy.

If you have followed the muscular movements, and thus rod movements, as described in the first few chapters, your loops will be nice and tight for maximum distance without being so tight that your fly catches on to the line at every cast. However, if you want to make a study of loop control, think back to your childhood. Did you ever make a whip out of a garden cane and a piece of string? I did, and great fun I had with it too, pretending I was in control of a Wells Fargo stagecoach being chased by Red Indians. I became an expert at cracking the whip over the ears of the horses, and when I became bored with that, I started to deadhead the roses, and then I graduated to daisy heads on the lawn. All I was doing was good practice for loop control – the ability to flick a fly line in a narrow loop using the same movements as I used as a child to pick daisy heads off with my piece of string.

Loop control is best practised with a fairly short line to start with. You will soon realise that the tighter the loop you want, the straighter the path of the rod tip has to be. Tight loops are created by driving the line in a straight line. Put a curve in the path of the rod tip and a wide loop is the inevitable result.

The man who does all his casting with the wrist is pivoting the rod around a fixed point, the wrist joint. The tip ring must be following the circumference of a circle, and a wide loop (and a sore wrist!) will be the consequence.

The man who does his casting with his arm extended above his head is pivoting the rod around a fixed point, the shoulder joint. The tip ring must be following the circumference of a circle, and a wide loop will be the consequence.

The man who puts a great deal of power into his casting is usually using a wide power arc. His rod is under power from perhaps 9.30 until 2.30. The tip ring is following a curved path, just like the rim of the clock face –uphill to 12 o'clock, then downhill to 2.30, and that curved track will result in a wide loop.

But surely we have already agreed that a wide loop yields more wind resistance, and that wind resistance is the major limiting factor in the distance the line will go? Greater increases in casting distance will result from narrowing the loop than can be achieved by altering anything else. It is worth practising loop control.

If you track your thumb in a straight line, the rod tip will track in a straight line, and your loops will be tight. Maximum distance for minimum effort will be your reward.

24
FLY LINES

It does seem slightly illogical to put a chapter on lines at the end of the book, but I do so to keep the technicalities until last.

When approaching fly fishing in a logical manner, one starts with the fly. That is the item to be presented to the fish and, ideally, the fish should see nothing else. A small fly can be cast with a lightweight tippet and leader. A large fly requires a stouter leader, not only to throw it, but to reduce the risk of breakage during casting, and while striking and playing the fish. It is a recipe for disaster to tie a size 8 longshank lead-headed lure on to the end of a tippet made of nylon which has a breaking strain of 4 lb. It is quite permissible to tie a size 14 nymph on to such a leader point.

The size of the fly therefore dictates the breaking strain of the leader. Small flies, say 16s, 14s and 12s, can be fished safely on a 4-lb tippet. Unleaded 10s and 8s can be fished safely on 6-lb nylon. Leaded 8s require 8-lb nylon for safety. Each time you change radically the size of fly, therefore, you should also change the tippet for one of a different breaking strain. But the solution does not end there.

I mentioned momentum in an earlier chapter. The force developed by a fly line is made up of its weight and velocity. There is considerable momentum generated on the strike – an AFTM 8 line jerked backwards when a fish takes the fly will impose a greater strain than would an AFTM 4 line jerked backwards at the same speed. It is important to match the size of the fly line to the strength of the tippet.

As a general rule, what I called the 'Rule of Numbers' in my book on stillwater fishing (*Flyfishing: Skill on Stillwaters*, 1990) should apply. Using an 8-lb leader, the line should be no heavier than an AFTM 8. Using a 4-lb leader, the line should be no heavier than AFTM 4. All anglers break this rule from time to time, but if they break the rule by more than two numbers, they will be in trouble. Set out below is a table which shows what I mean.

Size of fly	Tippet strength	Suggested line	Maximum line
16, 14, 12	4 lb	AFTM 4	AFTM 6
10, 8	6 lb	AFTM 6	AFTM 8
Leaded lures	8 lb	AFTM 8	AFTM 10
Small salmon flies	10 lb	AFTM 10	AFTM 12
Tubes	15 lb	AFTM 12	AFTM 12
Heavy tubes	20 lb	AFTM 12	AFTM 12

It will be noticed that I suggest only up to AFTM 12 for salmon fishing, and I do so because rods and lines heavier than this are not commonly available, and if they were, you would have to be a relative of Charles Atlas to wield them!

Equally at the other end of the scale there will be anglers who want to fish flies down to size 20, or to be very brave in rivers and streams with tippets down to 1½-lb breaking strain. They are fishing for very wary fish, and would normally use the lightest lines and rods they could find. For general fishing, however, I find that rods lighter than AFTM 4 are very delicate toys to play with.

The rod rating is dictated by the weight of the line, and while there is a great amount of latitude built into rods by reputable makers, you are asking for trouble to start with an AFTM 6 rod, put an AFTM 8 line on it, and then try to aerialise 15 yards. It might not break, but it will feel like a stick of spaghetti.

There are a few, a very few, rods available which will genuinely be able to handle a great range of line weights, but the action does change in the hand as the weight of line is increased or decreased, the timing of the cast will have to be varied, and the strike will have to be adjusted to cater for the risk of breakage – a stiff rod with a light line will have less shock-absorbing effect.

So much for the rule of numbers. We will now look at the AFTM scale itself, to understand the relationship between light lines and heavy lines.

	Weight of the first 30 ft, excluding the level tip		
AFTM number	In grains	In grams	In ounces
	Range	Nominal	Nominal
3	100 ± 6	6.48	0.228
4	120 ± 6	7.78	0.274
5	140 ± 6	9.07	0.32
6	160 ± 8	10.42	0.366
7	185 ± 8	11.99	0.422
8	210 ± 8	13.61	0.48
9	240 ± 10	15.55	0.55
10	280 ± 10	18.14	0.64
11	330 ± 12	21.38	0.75
12	380 ± 12	24.62	0.86

Careful study of this scale will reveal some interesting facts. For instance 10 yards of a DT 4 is about one-third the weight of 10 yards of DT 12. So the man trying to aerialise the whole of a DT 4 fly line is loading his rod with the equivalent of 10 yards of a DT 12. If he realised this, would he so abuse the rod on which he has spent several days' pay?

Another example is that the man aerialising 15 yards of a double-taper No. 8 line is putting at least 315 grains outside the tip ring – almost the weight of 10 yards of a No. 11. Would you think it reasonable to use a salmon line on your trout rod?

The key to avoiding the sort of overloading I am talking about is not to aerialise a lot of line, but to aerialise only as much as you need to make the spring work to maximum effectiveness, and to shoot any more line needed for the distance to the target. Shooting line does not overload a fly rod – aerialising extra line is what does the damage.

Let us now go back to basics, and talk about the manufacturing processes which put a fly line in your hands in the first place. If you read current advertising, you might be led to believe that most line manufacturers are working in a Stone-Age technology, and this is far from the case. Most line manufacturers spend huge sums of money in the research and testing of their fly lines before launching them upon the unsuspecting public. A modern fly line is the result of many years of evolution and is nearly always due to the efforts of dedicated anglers, good anglers, men whose pride and joy it is to produce the finest fly lines for fishing with. No gimmicks, no sudden blinding breakthroughs, just steady development with each stage well thought out and tested before the line is marketed.

The core of the fly line is nowadays constructed from man-made fibre. The days of silk, cotton or linen are long gone, as they all rotted in time, sometimes in a short time. Modern materials do not rot, and you can expect the core of a worn-out line to be as strong as when it was new.

The core is usually a braid of Terylene or similar material, as this has been found to give the best balance of properties. It will have a slight amount of give, or stretch, and the ability to bond well to the coating which will be applied over it, and to stay bonded throughout a great range of temperatures (from freezing to the temperature inside a car on a blazing hot day in Florida!). A finer braid is needed for light trout lines, and for weight-forward lines, but lines of over AFTM 9 usually have a heavier core, with a breaking strain of over 30 lb.

This core is run through a bath of molten plastic and out through a die which will expand and contract like the iris of a camera lens at regular intervals, so that the taper on the outside diameter is built in. Various devices to cool the plastic so that it sets, and a time delay for curing, are built into the manufacturing system, which is hundreds of yards long. (To save factory space, the line runs up and down towers on rollers, but the total distance the core travels is incredible.) The line is then cut at predetermined points so that the required profile of line is ready to be coiled.

Various treatments, such as a blast of cold air, or immersion in a water bath, are used to give a case-hardened effect to the plastic coating after it comes through the die, and there is sometimes a surface treatment as a last stage before cutting – a coat of silicone will make the line feel slick and smooth, and will give a greater distance of shoot (until it washes off in fishing!).

Which plastic is used for the coating is a matter of great attention. If the line is to be supple in all fishing temperatures, it tends to be soft on the surface, and is thus easily cut or damaged. If the line is given a hard surface, resistant to damage and wear, the line will feel hard, stiff, and unyielding, and may well have a memory of the reel coils, which re-asserts itself on the water. Catch 22, and this, whatever the plastic used, is the reason why fly lines have to represent a compromise. Some makers think that the angler wants a line which feels pleasant to handle. Some makers think anglers want a line which will last for a long time, and that feel is less important. Some makers think that anglers want a line which lies dead straight on the surface, and go to great lengths to ensure that the line is soft enough not to have a reel memory.

While on the subject of reel memory, consider that the standard trout fly reel has a diameter of 3–3½ inches. Some reels being advertised as giving less reel memory have a diameter of 4–4½ inches. If the line has a tendency for reel memory, does it really make any difference to you if the coils on the water are 3½ or 4½ inches across? Buy lines which have little or no tendency to retain reel memory rather than special reels to put dud lines on!

What you cannot see inside the fly line is one of its most important aspects, the bonding between core and coating. Some core materials are notoriously poor at allowing any plastic to bond to them. Some plastics are poor at bonding to anything anyway, whether or not a priming coat is inserted between the core and the coating. Beware the line which strips its coating too easily – it will cause you grief and aggravation, as I saw when in Florida a couple of years ago. A friend of mine, who had just bought the very latest line in technology, took the reel out of his car, threaded the rod, and ran some line between his hands to straighten it. The core/coating bond parted, and he ended up with what looked like a demented watch-spring. His language was terrible to hear, and it ruined his day's fishing.

There is even a difference of opinion on the desired smoothness of a fly line. One school of thought says that a highly polished, smooth surface will shoot through the rings best. The other school of thought says that a roughened surface touches the rings only on the bumps, thus giving less friction and farther shoot, and is more easily gripped when playing a fish! Take your pick, but my personal preference is for the smooth line. I believe the old engineering adage that noise means wear, and I do not like to hear line making a scraping noise as it shoots through the rings. I have not done any work on the comparisons, and am prepared to be persuaded, as my preference is purely gut-feel.

Some coatings are hydrophobic – they repel water. This is supposed to make them float higher, and thus be easier to pick up into a backcast, or be more visible on the water. If the level of water repellency is built into the plastic of the coating then fine, but beware the spray of silicone or wax polish which will wash off in half a day and, during the shelf life, may well have had a deleterious effect on the plastic so that it cracks after only half a season.

Finally we come to the knotty problem of line stretch. If you believe some of the advertising, stretchy lines feel like spaghetti, don't cast far, don't transmit the strike, and don't float very well. I wonder why anglers have been happy with them for the last 20 years? I recall many years ago, there was an article in *Salmon & Trout Magazine* extolling the virtues of a new kind of leader, invented by a Mr Elnetti in, I think, Vienna. The main bonus of this leader, made of a nylon braid, was that it acted as a shock absorber, and fewer fish were broken off on the strike! Some people in the UK jumped on the bandwaggon of profitability and started to push braided leaders for their shock-absorbing capability. Others pushed a rubbery elastic material, suggesting that it was a good idea to incorporate a foot of this stuff between line and leader. The poor angler became bamboozled by all the claims. Now we have fly lines being offered with stretch or non-stretch!

I have purely personal opinions of the non-stretch aspect of a fly line. I do not like it. I have never detected the slightest loss of distance because there was a tiny amount of give in my fly line. I have never failed to feel a take (providing I was concentrating and not looking up at an aeroplane!) because of the tiny amount of give in my fly line. On the other hand I am quite certain that I have caught fish which would have broken me if there had not been a little forgiveness in my fly line. It is all very well for the advertisements to say that two 180-lb men pulling at each end of a fly line can stretch it by several feet – of course they can. But the amount of pull exerted by the fly rod tip is measured in ounces, and the amount of stretch during casting is infinitesimal.

Have you ever tied a weight to the end of a piece of string and waved it back and forth? Have you ever tied the same weight to a piece of elastic and waved that? At first you find the weight keeps going away from you as the elastic stretches, then the elastic reaches its limit and accelerates the weight back at you. By the time it hits you between the eyes it is travelling very much faster than the weight on the non-stretch string would have been. I feel that there is a very strong possibility that a certain amount of stretch in a fly line may even *add* to the distance you can cast!

And whatever the advertisements say, I think that the choice of fly line for the average angler, after he has satisfied himself about colour, feel, slickness, and what his friends tell him about durability, comes down to price . . . just price. I know men who put 10-hours' wages into a fly line, and I think they are mad. They could buy a line, to all intents and purposes identical, for perhaps 2-hours' wages, and that, to me, represents much better value for money. If you are one of those people who think that nothing is really worth while unless it is the most expensive you can find, then great, buy it, and then reflect on all the advertising you are paying for! You are not paying for the fly line itself . . .

25
IN CONCLUSION

Happy is the man who can cast well. He gets an almost sensuous pleasure from seeing the line do exactly what he wants it to do. His fly lands lightly, scaring fewer fish. He can fish in places impossible for the man whose casting is restricted to a simple overhead cast. He catches more fish. He probably is part of the 10 per cent of anglers who catch 90 per cent of the fish. Seldom will he have to make excuses about the weather to justify an empty bag.

We have all heard the man say – 'I had a lovely day yesterday. I didn't catch anything, but I had a lovely day'. Usually this statement is greeted by a sardonic grin, and the suggestion that he would have had a damn sight better day if he had caught something, even if it was only one fish, because that is what he went for.

People go fishing to catch fish. They do not go fishing to watch the birdies, or commune with nature. Fish are the key. Please do not think that the sight of a kingfisher, the finding of a bird's nest, or a lovely sunset, do not make a memory – they do. But they are the icing on the cake, not the cake itself.

At the other end of the scale, I recall the occasion of a competition amongst the members of a local club, of which I was a member. On arrival at the water, the bailiff told us that he had stocked especially in honour of our competition, and I cursed him under my breath. The last thing I wanted to do was to catch lots of poor innocent stock fish, all the same size, and all with chewed tails. Of the 20 or so anglers out that evening, nearly all of us had the limit of four fish, all the same size, and in some places around the reservoir it had been a fish every cast. I became so bored that I deliberately walked a mile to the head of the reservoir and set myself the challenge of trying to catch a fish which was rising steadily at the limit of my casting ability. It took me 2 hours to catch that one fish, and I remember it more keenly than any of the others will remember their limit of stockies.

To the beginner, lots of fish means success, whether they were stocked yesterday or last year. After some experience, however, fishing that is too easy becomes boring, and lacks challenge. We go fishing for the challenge.

I was standing on the dam wall at Grafham once many years ago, and there were two friends fishing to my right. One man was catching nothing, and the other was landing a fish every 5 minutes. Finally the unsuccessful man called along to his companion, 'Jack, what fly are you using?' The answer came back in a flash, 'I don't know the name of it, but these damned fish are interrupting my casting rhythm'.

Which brings us back to casting, which is a challenge in itself. The mastery of casting will add more pleasure to your fishing than anything else I can suggest. A casting lesson will be more useful than all the rods you might buy, will give more pleasure than a week of day-tickets on some hotshot reservoir, and will stand you in better stead for your old age than all the books or all the video tapes. Books and video tapes cannot look at you and tell you what you are doing wrong. A good instructor can, and will.

I believe it was Sam Goldwyn who said – 'If you want to send a message, use Western Union'. He was, of course, talking about films, not fly fishing. I want to send you a message about fly fishing, so I will put it into this book with a clear conscience.

If you do decide to have a lesson from a person who gives casting lessons, I most earnestly suggest that you check first whether he is a member of the Association of Professional Game Angling Instructors, APGAI for short. If he is, ask him whether he is qualified in the subject you wish to cover – it is no good going to a fly-tying member if you want to learn a double-Spey cast. If he is so qualified, you can be assured that your instruction will be of the highest standard available in this country.

I regret to say that there are quite a lot of people setting themselves up as casting instructors as a result of being made redundant from their jobs, or from the feeling that they have fished for many years and they might as well earn some pocket money from their hobby. Nice men, most of them, but would you go to a totally unqualified person for medical or dental treatment, or legal advice? In a lifetime, most of us spend more on our fishing than we do on any of these professions, so why not get properly qualified tuition – it will be cheaper in the long run, as you will not have to unlearn any of the faults you may pick up.

If you get Uncle Joe to teach you, because he has fished all his life, you will learn all his faults, and will then build in some extra ones of your own. By the time you realise that something is really wrong, you will have created muscle memory for some habits which will be hard to break.

By all means read this book. As a substitute for a lesson, face to face, I have done my best to set out for you what are the faults to look for, what is the easy way to cast, what the theory of it all is. At least if you know what you are trying to achieve, you are off to a flying start.

Practise your casting. You do not even need to have a rod in your hand – you can do it while you are sitting in front of a boring television programme. Start with the rod down. Bend the elbow until the rod comes up to 10 o'clock. Flick to 12.30. Thumb no higher than your ear? Good. Wrist not cocked? Good. Wait for it to straighten out behind, then stick your thumb in his eye. Drift down. You have just practised an overhead cast and, if you do that often enough, you will have built in muscle memory for a nice cast, so that when you put a rod in that hand, it will seem automatic, and you can concentrate on what the line is doing.

May all your casts land where you want them to, and gently. Tight lines and screaming reels to you.

INDEX

Numbers in *italic* refer to illustrations